GRACE UNTAMED

GRACE UNTAMED

A 60-DAY DEVOTIONAL

Edited by

ELYSE FITZPATRICK

transforming lives together

GRACE UNTAMED
Published by David C Cook
4050 Lee Vance View
Colorado Springs, CO 80918 U.S.A.

David C Cook Distribution Canada
55 Woodslee Avenue, Paris, Ontario, Canada N3L 3E5

David C Cook U.K., Kingsway Communications
Eastbourne, East Sussex BN23 6NT, England

The graphic circle C logo is a registered trademark of David C Cook.

Unless otherwise noted, all Scripture quotations are taken from The
Holy Bible, English Standard Version® (ESV®), copyright © 2001
by Crossway, a publishing ministry of Good News Publishers. Used
by permission. All rights reserved. Scripture quotations marked NIV
are taken from the Holy Bible, New International Version®, NIV®.
Copyright © 1973, 2011 by Biblica, Inc.® Used by permission of
Zondervan. All rights reserved worldwide. www.zondervan.com; KJV
are taken from the King James Version of the Bible. (Public Domain.)

LCCN 2015959523
ISBN 978-0-7814-1455-5
eISBN 978-1-4347-1044-4

© 2016 TT, Inc.

The Team: Alex Field, Ingrid Beck, Jared C. Wilson, Amy
Konyndyk, Tiffany Thomas, Karen Athen, Susan Murdock
Cover Design: Nick Lee

Printed in the United States of America
First Edition 2016

1 2 3 4 5 6 7 8 9 10

121815

CONTENTS

INTRODUCTION

This book is a collection of short devotionals about God's grace, that is, *His generous favor bestowed on the undeserving* through Christ. This collection is spoken to you through a myriad of voices—voices of believers who have walked with Jesus long enough to know that any progress they make toward holiness in this life is progress accomplished through grace *alone*. They have all discovered at a deep level that their walk with the Lord was not only initiated by His gracious intervention interrupting their selfish course of life, but also that their continuance in this life of faith is accomplished by His sheer determination to sustain them in it—no matter how slow-footed or selfish they remain.

In one of the best-known passages about grace, Paul described this untamed and untamable disposition of God toward us.

> For the grace of God has appeared, bring-
> ing salvation for all people, training us to
> renounce ungodliness and worldly passions,
> and to live self-controlled, upright, and
> godly lives in the present age, waiting for our
> blessed hope, the appearing of the glory of

our great God and Savior Jesus Christ, who
gave himself for us to redeem us from all law-
lessness and to purify for himself a people for
his own possession who are zealous for good
works. (Titus 2:11–14)

Like the rest of the contributors to this book, I have discovered how desperate I am for His grace—not just at the
beginning of my walk but even now, nearly a half century later.
I remain desperate for a grace that transforms and trains me,
freeing me from desires that have enslaved me, freeing me to
live a self-controlled, godly life now. And like every contrib-
utor, I long to live a life that is marked more and more by
holiness, by His gracious training, by true zeal. This can only
be accomplished by His powerful working in me through His
unstoppable favor.

This book is about being trained by grace, a process
accomplished through faith in the gracious truth that I am
fully known yet deeply loved, warmly welcomed, completely
forgiven, and eternally adopted through His work alone. Faith
in His work and not my own, in His righteousness and not
my own, has eventuated in a tangible transformation of my
life. That's not to say that there aren't days (and many of them

in a row) when I know that all I'm doing is slogging it out, when my walk stinks of two wretched steps forward and three unbelieving slips back. But then … thankfully, there are other days when I discover, to my great surprise, that situations that used to send me into self-pity, anger, or fear no longer have any hold on me. I think that's the training God does by grace. He teaches me the truth that I already have "all things" in Christ and that, because I have them and Him, and because He belongs to His Father, I no longer have to fight or fear. His grace is teaching me to believe that "all things are yours, whether … the world or life or death or the present or the future—all are yours, and you are Christ's, and Christ is God's" (1 Cor. 3:21–23).

You'll find that each of the contributors to this collection of devotions about grace is just like you: striving to respond to His gracious training and yet tripping and then falling over and over again into His gracious arms of mercy, only to get up again (by grace) and try again tomorrow. No one who has contributed to this book about grace has even scratched the surface of the depths of God's love and patience with us. But we're looking there, we're longing to understand, and we're praying for "strength to comprehend" the love of Christ (Eph. 3:18–19) that yet remains incomprehensible to us.

Thank you for joining us in praying that we will have faith to believe that His grace really can, after all, train us in godliness. His grace is untamed. It has no boundaries. It is profligate and unstoppable. And it is powerful to train all who believe.

YOU ARE LOVED ... NO, REALLY

by Elyse Fitzpatrick

See what kind of love the Father has given to us.

1 John 3:1

How would you live today if you knew at the very bottom of your soul that you were loved? You know what that would do? It would free you from having to make sure you were being loved. How much chasing after being loved have you done? How much effort have you poured into your pursuit of being loved?

God's one-way love for us is the only love that can free us from our incessant pursuit of the love of others. We must be done with all that! I'll tell you why: because no matter how many people you get to love you, it will never be enough. Let me remind you of Haman in the book of Esther. Haman had everyone in the entire city bowing down to him when he rode by, but it wasn't enough. He didn't have Mordecai's worship, and it drove him crazy. Even though we can see the stupidity of Haman's deadly desire, you and I act the same way. It doesn't matter how much we are loved by others; it never totally satisfies because the holes in our hearts weren't meant to be filled by anything other than a perfect love—the love of God.

But here's the good news: through the gospel, we get to be free from that slavery. We've been loved by Somebody who knows our hearts, who sees every dark and doubtful thing within them. And yet *He loves us* and He gives Himself for us.

God's grace liberates us from this kind of gluttony for love. I don't need to seek endlessly and fruitlessly to be loved anymore. The perfect love of Christ has satisfied my need and driven out my fear.

Thought to Remember for Today

You are already more loved than you could ever dare hope. This love didn't come to you because you are wonderful; it isn't something you earned by your good behavior. That's really great news, because if God's love were something we could earn by our good behavior, then His love would be something we could lose by our bad behavior. God's love rests on us because of His gracious choice of us in Christ, and that love is indestructible.

LOVED BECAUSE OF HIS WORK

by Elyse Fitzpatrick

*Who shall bring any charge against God's
elect? It is God who justifies.*

Romans 8:33

The Father looks at us and smiles upon us. Why? Is it because we got up early this morning and did our devotions? No. He likes that we did that, sure, but He's smiling upon us because Jesus Christ lived perfectly in our place. We are loved at every moment of the day, regardless of our behavior. Not only that—we are *justified*. Do you know what this means? It's amazing. It means we don't have to justify ourselves to God, to ourselves, or to anyone else ever again.

The justification in Christ we receive by faith is an incredible double blessing. It means first that I am forgiven "just as if I'd never sinned." This is great news! But justification is not simply about having a blank slate. No, there's another great blessing. We have a clean record, yes, but justification also means "just as if I'd always obeyed." God takes our newly blank slate and writes on it the perfect obedience of Jesus! So when God the Father looks at me, He says, "This is My beloved daughter, in whom I am well pleased."

Grace reminds us over and over again that when God looks upon us, He smiles because He no longer sees our sin. In fact, instead He sees the perfect record of His Son. Now we don't need to protect ourselves or seek to justify ourselves anymore. God has promised to care for us so we don't have to worry that we'll mess up His plan or miss His will. We've been given everything in Christ, so in response to that, we can pursue godliness, knowing that although we need continual pardon, we already have it. It's a done deal.

Here's an example from my own life: I get up in the morning and I pray, "My Father who art in heaven, hallowed be Thy name. Glorify Yourself. Let Your kingdom come, and let Your will be done by me today." And then I get to the end of the day, and I look back and see all the ways I failed. At that point, I can choose to say, "I'm going to get up tomorrow and do better," or I can throw myself on the mercy of Christ and flee to Him and thank Him for my justification.

One-way love brings that kind of freedom to us. Only God's grace does that. It makes us honest about our failures and frees us from our self-justifying and self-condemning inclinations.

Thought to Remember for Today

As you think about your Christian experience, how much has the truth of justification by faith impacted your daily life? Perhaps for you this beautiful truth has had a great impact, or perhaps not. The really great news is that even if justification hasn't been the pivot point of your faith, your Father still sees you as completely sinless and completely obedient.

CHRIST'S TRANSFORMING LOVE

by Elyse Fitzpatrick

*As indeed he says in Hosea, "Those who were not
my people I will call 'my people,' and her who
was not beloved I will call 'beloved.'"*

Romans 9:25

When you really live in the light of the gospel, it transforms your obedience. Because of God's love, your obedience is no longer a burden. That's not to say we don't fight to believe and obey—we do. But the kind of love that comes to us through the suffering of Christ—and the raising of Christ—*transforms* our obedience. See, as long as my obedience is focused on me and how I'm working my way down the road of sanctification, no matter how hard I try, I will not find within myself the desire, the motivation, the power to pursue true godliness with longevity.

When I put my eyes on my own performance, in a way it's like seeing myself as God's foster child. As a foster child, I have to walk on eggshells and make sure not to break any of the family rules. I think that too often we all view ourselves as God's foster children, and we're not sure why He would choose us. But then the message of the true gospel breaks through: He's *adopted* us! God has made us one of His very own.

We have to begin to see ourselves as sons and daughters with whom the Lord is well pleased. But how do we do this? We do it through the work of our big brother Jesus. Listen to this passage from Romans:

> As indeed he says in Hosea, "Those who were not my people I will call 'my people,' and her who was not beloved I will call 'beloved.' And in the very place where it was said to them, 'You are not my people,' there they will be called 'sons of the living God.'" (Rom. 9:25–26)

That's who we are! Once we were not called "beloved," but now we're called "beloved." Once we were not called His children, but now by faith in Jesus Christ we are. The Son of God lived perfectly in our place, died our death, and rose again for us, breaking the power of the curse of death. And in this work, He forever measures up on our behalf. When we trust in Him, His perfect obedience becomes ours. He's done all this for you so that you can say, today, "I am His beloved child."

Thought to Remember for Today

Those amazing words of adoption, first spoken through the prophet Hosea and later reiterated by Paul, are meant to free us from the fear that we will out-sin God's love and welcome. Rather than living like foster children, let's live like dearly loved sons and daughters. Let's obey, yes, but as children, as those who cannot be disowned or turned away.

LIBERATED FROM FEAR, GUILT, AND MERIT

by Elyse Fitzpatrick

There is no fear in love, but perfect love casts out fear. For fear has to do with punishment, and whoever fears has not been perfected in love. We love because he first loved us.

1 John 4:18–19

We have been liberated from the bondage of "fear of punishment." First John 4:18 tells us there is no fear in love. The gospel logic goes like this: if you're still afraid He's going to punish you, you haven't yet soaked your soul in His love.

Christian, let this sink in: He loves you—you have nothing to fear.

Your obedience to the Father no longer has to be motivated by guilt. Grace cleanses us from guilt, which will never motivate true obedience. Sure, we can be motivated by guilt to outwardly conform—because we want to be able to feel good about ourselves or approve of ourselves or have other people approve of us. But if you are obeying so you can feel free from guilt, you're obeying for *you*, really, and not for God. True obedience only happens in the context of love for Christ and what He's already done.

Grace also removes merit as a motive for obedience. So you can stop working to earn God's favor. Now, I didn't say, "You can stop working." But you can definitely stop working to "measure up." If you want to motivate me to lay down my life, please tell me what Christ has done for me, tell me that all the merit I ever needed is already mine.

Imagine Jesus when He was a little boy. Let's say His sister takes a block of wood and bonks Him on the head. Let's say His brothers tease Him. At every opportunity, He's responding to them in love. And do you know what He's doing in those moments? He's earning *your* merit.

Please don't insult the perfect work of Jesus by thinking that everything He did was merely some sort of example. His behavior was a great example; we could find no better role model than Jesus. But Jesus did not come to simply be our role model. He came to be our Savior. And to be our Savior, He became our righteousness. He became our merit. In Christ, we are set free from so much!

Thought to Remember for Today

The beautiful, liberating truth of one-way love is that it frees us from the fear of punishment, from faith-sapping guilt, and from the merry-go-round of merit. For those who have put their faith in the Son, punishment is no longer an option for God. Guilt is vanquished because our slate is wiped clean. And all the merit that ever needed to be earned has already been deposited into our account in heaven.

Day 5

BELOVED, DEAR CHILDREN

by Scotty Smith

Son of man, these men have set up idols in their hearts....
I will do this to recapture the hearts of the people of Israel.
Ezekiel 14:3, 5 NIV

God's word through Ezekiel was, "I will do this."

Don't you wish that, at the very moment we were justified by grace alone through faith alone, idolatry were no longer an issue? Our great hope is that we will not always be idolaters. One day we will be as lovely and as loving as Jesus, because God does not lie and He will bring His covenant to completion. So we can relax and go under the surgery of the One committed to our freedom, the One who said, "I will do this."

Paul wrote in 1 Corinthians 10:14, "Therefore, *my* beloved, flee from idolatry." John wrote, "*Dear* children, keep yourselves from idols" (1 John 5:21 NIV). "Dear children." "My beloved." This is how both Paul and John exhort us to fight idolatry: *we are beloved children* whom God has promised to liberate. It's this relationship that enables us to be honest about the fact that we give our hearts and our energies to things that are not God. Only those who know themselves to be fully and eternally accepted in Jesus have the motivation and moxie to do this hard—and heart—work.

Here is the heart work God has done in my life. Several devastating events intersected with my sinful nature and produced a whole pantheon of false gods. The first of the two most formative events was that I was sexually molested when I was an eight-year-old boy. Honestly, it wasn't until about nine years ago that I gained an awareness of how devastating and shaming that was for me. And even though I knew Jesus was my righteousness and that He took my guilt, I never knew that He took my shame, too.

The second part of my story is that my mother was killed in a car wreck when I was eleven. One hour after I learned of my mother's death, my father arrived at the home of the people who were caring for my brother and me. The door opened and he asked, "Boys, do you know what has happened?" My brother and I answered yes. With that he walked right by us, and my mom's name was not mentioned for the next thirty-nine years. In many ways, the death of my mom really represents a dark vortex, an intersection where my sinful nature and these profound wounds came into focus for me. Out of this deep pain came idolatries that I have dealt with for years.

It's only as I have grown in knowing that I was the "beloved," a "dear child," that I have been able to have the courage to look at my woundedness and rest in Christ's welcome of beloved sinners, even those who build idols right in the middle of their pain.

Thought to Remember for Today

It is only as we learn how loved we are that we can face our wounds. It is only when we know that God will free us that we are free to survey the idols that grow in those dark, bruised places. Yes, today I am a free man, and continually becoming freer, all because of the grace of God. I cannot do the hard work of seeking out and destroying my idols … and neither can you do that with yours. This is work Jesus does. He said, "I will do this." You can trust Him today.

A JOURNEY OF SELF-SALVATION

by Scotty Smith

*I will give him a white stone, with a new name written on
the stone that no one knows except the one who receives it.*

Revelation 2:17

At the age of eleven I knew I needed salvation, but it wasn't a relationship with God that I was thinking about. I began a journey of
self-salvation, looking for deliverance, safety, and security, trying
to make sense of life on my own. I tried to become my own savior.
I was a young boy, and I had a deep longing for comfort. Can the
quest for comfort be an idol? Of course! It was something in my
heart, a screaming emptiness, a sense of utter loneliness. I would
go to bed at night and hear my father wail at the far end of the
house, and I'd put a pillow over my head because it sounded like
a banshee cry. I desperately wanted comfort, but there was none
to be had.

So here's where I went to begin worshipping the god of
comfort: I came home from school one day and stared at the
cookie jar. With no premeditation, I simply pulled out the front

of my T-shirt, poured in a whole jarful of chocolate chip cookies, and sat down in front of *The Flintstones*. As I started eating those cookies, there was a sense in that moment that life might be okay. Food became something that offered me a payoff. It gave me comfort. I didn't know where else to go, but I felt comforted for the moment.

Fast-forward to the ninth grade, and I was portly and I'd earned the nickname "Meatball." In the first week of high school, with a few of my posse hanging with me, I was petrified when the head football coach came toward me. I hoped this would be a good thing. He was a neighbor, I cut his grass, and my dad worked with his brother. I thought, *If the head coach knows my name, my friends will see and be impressed.*

Coach walked up to me, and I was expecting, "Scotty, how are you doing?" Instead he looked me right in the eyes and said, "I would be so ashamed if I had a body like yours." Then he walked right on by. It was as if the man had taken a chainsaw to my soul.

I was shamed. It was bad enough that this man would say those words to me, but I had already been shamed by the abuse I suffered as a young boy. As these shames piled up, I began to question myself, even wondering things like, "Am I a man?" I wondered what these things done and said to me might mean for my very identity and worth. And even as I'm tempted to seek significance and comfort in all sorts of things, I have realized the only real comfort from and silencer of shame is what the King of Creation says about me.

Thought to Remember for Today

As you read over the description of some of the idols that grew out of my woundedness, are you able to see the wounds and idols you struggle with? The good news of the gospel is that no one has the right to name you or to force you into some identity from the past. Jesus has given you a new name, and He has written it forever on His hands. You are not your history. You are not what others have done to you or said about you. You are Christ's.

WEAK SUBSTITUTES FOR A SAVIOR

by Scotty Smith

Therefore, my beloved, flee from idolatry.

1 Corinthians 10:14

The next idol in my life began to rear its ugly head. It was control. After the coach's crushing words, I got desperate to fix myself. I hated to exercise, but with no one coaching me, after school I would come home to my empty house, wrap my body in cellophane, put on sweats, and run. I was trying to save myself, really, and for three months I ate heads of lettuce and drank water and ended up dropping forty pounds. When I started my tenth-grade year, my nickname had become "Skinny Scotty," and while I was in great danger of having an eating disorder, I was more concerned about appearing in control. *I'll show him,* I thought about the coach.

Even though I was still ragingly insecure, Skinny Scotty had a new way of comforting himself. I wasn't changed at all on the inside; I had just put another false god in the temple of my heart.

Yes, I still wanted comfort, but now I also worshipped control. Exercise became a religion, a way to control what people said about me. But even this wasn't enough for my idolatrous heart. I also wanted community, acceptance. I discovered a category in the yearbook called "Best Dressed," and I began to earn money so I could buy clothes. I got two part-time jobs, and I started stealing.

This focus gave way to a longing for impact and significance. I wanted people to notice me.

I joined my brother's band. I was so insecure, so disconnected. I had a closet full of clothes. I would buy three of the same thing so nothing I wore would ever look worn out. Desperate people do desperate things. Then, as I was preparing to drive to the first gig the band had, I heard that the only girl with whom I'd had any kind of relationship had just been killed in a car accident.

Soon, in His grace and kindness, the Lord brought me to Himself and I became a serious Christian. I began to learn and study, but in so many ways I was still trying to satisfy my idols of comfort, control, acceptance, and significance—only now by filtering them through religion. But even religion was no substitute for the Savior, and my religious devotion was no substitute for my deliverance from idols. I needed the grace of God.

Thought to Remember for Today

As you've read over this candid confession of god-making, have you sensed that you can be freed from your own pain and resultant idolatries? Knowing others are just like us is very comforting, but knowing that Jesus knows us and is filled with mercy is even more liberating. Let's face it: God only has wounded idolaters to work with. It's all He has, but He's got one perfect Son whose faithfulness becomes ours by grace. Remember that even in your idolatry you're still called, "My beloved."

THE DIFFICULTY OF RELATIONSHIPS

by Paul David Tripp

*For the love of Christ controls us, because we have concluded
this: that one has died for all, therefore all have died; and
he died for all, that those who live might no longer live for
themselves but for him who for their sake died and was raised.*

2 Corinthians 5:14–15

Why in the world are marriages so hard? Why are relationships and friendships so difficult? Why is parenting so tough? We all know every sort of relationship is hard, don't we? I mean, you have never had a relationship in your life that hasn't disappointed you in some way. Isn't that incredible? Not one. What's *that* about?

Look at 2 Corinthians 5:14–15. In this passage Paul gave a defense of his ministry. "And he died for all"—now pay very careful attention—"that"—the word *that* introduces a purpose statement—"those who live might no longer live for themselves but for him who for their sake died and was raised."

I don't know what you've thought about this passage, but this is the ultimate diagnostic of why relationships can be such a struggle, why they can be so hurtful, so dysfunctional. How can it be that this person I once adored, this person whose voice would lift my heart, this person with whom I felt such community, can make me so angry, so distressed? How is it that we can have so much tension between us that you couldn't cut it with a knife—you'd have to use a chainsaw? Why?

Well, here's what 2 Corinthians 5:15 says to me: Sin causes all of us to shrink our worlds down to the claustrophobic confines of our wants, our needs, our feelings. Sin is self-obsessed, self-focused. Sin inserts *me* in the center of my world—the one place I must never be. Sin makes me full of myself. Sin makes it all about me. Sin makes me a vat of selfish thoughts and desires and wants. I want to drive on roads paid for by other citizens who choose not to use them. I want a wife who says, "Of course, Paul, I agree with you; I've lived with the glory that is you." I want children who say, "I will forthwith go and obey, oh wise father whom I've been given." I want neighbors who moved into the neighborhood just because I'm there.

What can disrupt this idolatry of self? What can help us bring healing and grace to our relationships? Paul says it's the work of Jesus. He forgives us and frees us, and by this good news, we get out of the center of our lives and revolve around Him.

Thought to Remember for Today

Every one of us knows what it's like to be in a relationship that's gone south. And we all know the reason is because we want what we want so desperately. The good news for all of us is that Jesus brings not only the forgiveness of sins to men and women who have selfishly ruined relationships, but He also is flooding our hearts with His love, which will enable us to live selflessly every day.

THE DNA OF SIN IS SELFISHNESS

by Paul David Tripp

For the love of Christ controls us, because we have concluded this: that one has died for all, therefore all have died; and he died for all, that those who live might no longer live for themselves but for him who for their sake died and was raised.

2 Corinthians 5:14–15

Once again the apostle Paul actually argued that the DNA of sin is selfishness. You don't have to look very far to see this. Have you ever seen a young child, who can't even speak yet, stiffen up in anger? You've fed this child, you've changed his diapers, you've bathed him, you've sung him every song and read him every story, but just you try to put him to bed and leave the room. You hear a scream behind you. He has pushed himself up, body stiffening, brow furrowed. Guess what he's saying? "Oh no you don't! You will not leave! I am the lord!"

You might laugh at that notion, but this is only evidence of the selfishness of sin that lies in each one of us from conception. And there is untold human relational carnage that comes from this—the deepest of angers, the deepest of hurts, the deepest of divisions.

Sin is fundamentally antisocial. At creation, mankind was hardwired to live both an upward and an outward life—upward in submissive worship of God, outward in self-sacrificial love of neighbor. But sin turns us in on ourselves. Sin is a sadly dysfunctional, *inward* way of life.

Now, if the DNA of sin is selfishness, and if that means sin is fundamentally antisocial, it means we end up dehumanizing the people in our lives. No longer are they objects of affection. They get reduced to vehicles or obstacles. They're vehicles helping us get what we want—"I love you; I need you; but if you stand in the way of what I want, I'm spontaneously angry and I want to do you emotional harm."

If you don't think that applies to you, let me ask you this question: How much of your anger in relationships over the past month had anything whatsoever to do with the kingdom of God? *Own* it. Own it: we're angry because someone's in the way of what we want.

Thought to Remember for Today

None of us is excused from having to own that we are angry and that we frustrate relationships because we don't get what we want. The only truth that will free us from our incessant self-centeredness is the truth that Jesus died for these very sins. Today, as you consider the patterns of selfishness that mark your relationships, ask the Spirit to remind you of the great truths of the gospel that are also true about you: you are loved and forgiven.

GRACE LIBERATES YOU FROM YOU
by Paul David Tripp

For the love of Christ controls us, because we have concluded
this: that one has died for all, therefore all have died; and
he died for all, that those who live might no longer live for
themselves but for him who for their sake died and was raised.

2 Corinthians 5:14–15

I am my greatest relational problem—me. And your biggest problem is you. Now, don't misunderstand me. I know you'll be sinned
against; I know people suffer abuse of all kinds; but my greatest and
deepest difficulty in relationships actually exists inside of me and
not outside of me. That's why Paul offered the cure when he said
Jesus came to rescue you from *you*.

Grace alone changes the whole relational paradigm, our
whole lifestyle of inward-bentness. Grace liberates you from
you, so you can actually have a thing that could be described as
a relationship.

Grace frees you from three things. First, grace frees you
from your bondage to self-righteousness. You see, if your hope

and security in life are placed in the basket of *your* righteousness, it is hard to maintain a relationship. It's hard to live with you, because you cannot be wrong. But God gives you, in His Son, a righteousness that's not your own. And once you get that it's not about you but about Christ, and once you know that as you stand as righteous before God you are free to own up to being a bit of a mess, you don't have to be so defensive about everything or get your own way.

Second, embracing Christ's righteousness as your own gives you freedom from needing to be in control. Jesus said this: "Fear not, little flock, for it is your Father's good pleasure to give you the kingdom" (Luke 12:32). It's not you trying to construct a kingdom of your own and placing your hope in it. You've already got more than you could ever want in God's kingdom, so your arguing and your angling can be put to rest.

Third, Christ's righteousness frees you from bondage to unrealistic expectations. You stop seeking horizontally what is only supplied vertically; you stop asking the people in your life to be your own personal messiahs, who will make you feel good about yourself, give you meaning and purpose, make you happy.

Grace says we've already been given everything we need for life and godliness. It's all ours in Christ.

Thought to Remember for Today

The beautiful truth of the righteousness that has been imputed to us by Christ is the only truth powerful enough to free us from all our selfishness and our desire to be made much of. This glorious reality is for you today. You can live in the light of all Jesus has done to free you from yourself.

Day 11

THE NOW-ISM OF THE GOSPEL

by Paul David Tripp

His divine power has granted to us all things
that pertain to life and godliness.

2 Peter 1:3

Notice the two words Peter used in 2 Peter 1:3: *life* and *godliness*. Why did he use these two words? Because he knew his audience. If he said just "everything for life," we'd say, "Well, yeah, we get everything we need for eternal life." Now, that's a wonderful thing, but that's not what he's really talking about. So he added *godliness*. By God's divine power, I've been given everything I need—oh, this is glorious!—to be what I'm supposed to be and to do what I'm supposed to do in the place where God has placed me right now.

What's godliness? It's a God-honoring life between the time I first come to Christ and the time I finally go home to be with Him. For the rescue of our relationships we must embrace the *now-ism* of the gospel of the Lord Jesus Christ. Second Peter 1:3 tells me that *right now* I have everything I need for godliness. I don't look to others for my hope, identity, energy, or acceptance. I already have them in Christ. And I can lift that burden off the shoulders of those with whom I relate. They're not my saviors—I free them in the name of Jesus. How beautiful is that?

The work of Christ was given to us in an instant—that's justification—but it is taken on and acquired by us in a process—that's sanctification. So, in a way, we are both free and in need of being freed. I still have places where I hang on to my defective righteousness and have to be right. There are still places where I make it all about my kingdom and have to be in control, where I still place unrealistic expectations on the people in my life. And so I celebrate the grace I've been given and I pray for further liberation.

Welcome to your relational world, a world of the already and the not yet. Thank God that His gospel meets us and works for us at every point on the eternal timeline! That's the now-ism of the gospel.

Thought to Remember for Today

So here's what you do: At the beginning of each day, starting today, pray these three things: (1) "God, I am a person in desperate need of help this morning." (2) "I pray that in Your grace You will send Your helpers my way." (3) "I pray that when the help comes, You will give me the humility to receive it with joy."

Day 12

JUST BE NORMAL

by Steve Brown

*For freedom Christ has set us free; stand firm therefore,
and do not submit again to a yoke of slavery.*

Galatians 5:1

Read Matthew 12:1–8.

Now I want to tell you something radical: if you're going to be free, it means being *normal*. Jesus's disciples were hungry. They weren't trying to make a statement or an obscene gesture to the Pharisees. They weren't saying, "We are free—look at us!" They were simply hungry and they ate the grain. In today's world, people standing around would object to their eating by saying something like, "You can't eat that. It will make you fat and give you cancer." But Jesus would respond to those little-"l" laws the same way He responded to the big-"L" law the Pharisees were concerned about. He would tell them they had it all wrong.

Many of us have this really stupid idea that if we don't seem like we have it all together, we will hurt our witness. Let me tell you something: this doesn't help your witness. Nobody's ever drawn to Christ by people who pretend to be something they're not. Instead, they're drawn to Christ when they see how messy you are and how honest you are, and yet how much at the same time you enjoy the love of Jesus and trust in Him rather than appearances. Yes, if you do this, you might end up living your life in such a way that uptight Christians doubt your salvation, but people who enjoy grace and people who desperately want grace will be attracted to you, and you will look normal.

The point? Be who you are. And I think that's what was going on in Matthew 12. The disciples were hungry, so they got some food and they ate; and the Pharisees went ballistic.

Here's what Martin Luther had to say about that kind of religion in his treatise on Christian liberty: "Use your freedom constantly and consistently ... despite the tyrants and the stubborn, so they may learn that they are impious, that their law and works are of no avail for righteousness, and that they had no right to set them up."[1]

Thought to Remember for Today

Many of us think we can win others to Christ by being punctilious and overly strict with ourselves. But neither Jesus the Savior nor

Martin Luther the Reformer would agree. What draws people to Christ aren't your multitudinous rules and straitlaced life but rather the one-way love of Jesus, who loves to save and welcome sinners.

PROVIDING COMFORT LIKE HEAVEN

by Steve Brown

But if we walk in the light, as he is in the light, we have
fellowship with one another, and the blood of Jesus his
Son cleanses us from all sin. If we say we have no sin,
we deceive ourselves, and the truth is not in us.

1 John 1:7–8

Maybe you should live your life so the Pharisees will doubt your salvation. And you should ask some brothers and sisters to hold you accountable—not to be a wonderful, nice, everything-put-together Christian faker but against being an uptight religious sourpuss. You need Christian friends to hold you accountable to bask in your freedom to the glory of God.

I was once speaking at a church in our city, and I told those folks that smoking my pipe is kind of like heaven for me. If I'm preaching a sermon that just seems to be awful and I feel like I'm doing a terrible job, I tell myself that if I can just get through it to the end, I can go home and smoke my pipe. It's like heaven.

The next time I was at that church, I was standing at the door in the back, and guys were putting cigars in my pocket! I brought home, I bet you, fifty to sixty cigars that day. It was such a great comfort. I had told them smoking a pipe was like a reminder of the comfort of heaven, and they wanted to make sure I had as much comfort as I could get in the here and now. That's what those in the church do for each other—provide the reminders of the comfort of heaven.

You know, the world is bad. I've buried more babies and cleaned up after more suicides and listened to more confessions than I can even remember. This is not a place for sissies. It's really, really hard. And we're not home yet. But we can remind each other of the freedom we have in Christ, providing one another with a comfort akin to heaven.

Thought to Remember for Today

The wonderful news about our true home, heaven, is that it will be a place where we'll never have to pretend. We'll never have to be properly perfect because we will already be made perfect by His work in us. The fellowship we have together as believers is not a fellowship of perfect religiosity, but rather a fellowship around the truth that we are forgiven.

NO ROOM FOR GOTCHAS

by Steve Brown

For freedom Christ has set us free; stand firm therefore,
and do not submit again to a yoke of slavery.

Galatians 5:1

One problem Pharisees have is they're always looking for sin. But you don't really have to look for sin. It's everywhere. Looking for sin, even in your church, is like being a mosquito at a nudist colony—you know where to look; the real problem is knowing where to start!

Norm Evans, my professional football player friend, told a story about a college lineman who came to the coach and said, "The opposing lineman keeps pulling my helmet down over my eyes. What should I do?" And his coach said, "Son, don't let him." Pharisees are looking for sin in you, and they're going to pull a "Gotcha!" on you all the time. Don't let them. That's what it means to live in the freedom of grace.

Another thing we notice about the Pharisees of the Bible is that not only were they looking for sin but when they found it,

they couldn't be consistent with it. In Matthew 12 when they
tried to play gotcha over the disciples eating grain on the Sabbath,
Jesus essentially said, "We're eating because we're hungry. Don't
you remember David and the priests who broke the law all the
time? What's wrong with you guys?" Pharisees are never consistent. They only play gotcha with others when it's in their own
best interest.

And we have our equivalent in the evangelical Christian sub-
culture. We're so uptight about our rules. Some of us don't dance
because we think it'll always lead to sex. Or we warn people off
movies because we think if someone goes to a PG-rated movie
one week, they'll be going to an R-rated movie the next week and
eventually engaging in pornography. So we put rules on everything because we think rules will stop us from sinning.

Don't let the Pharisees multiply rules in your life. Don't let
them convince you that rules will keep you from sinning. You'll
never be able to keep everything together like they tell you to, and
trying certainly won't help you live a holy life. Own your sin and
hand it to Jesus. He will set you free from both sin and the rules
that don't help you but actually condemn you.

Thought to Remember for Today

Even though it seems counterintuitive, multiplying rules so that we fence off the possibility of sin is actually the greatest deterrent to holy living there is. If our goal is a holy life, then we need to press into the truths of the gospel—that we are already loved and forgiven and that the law no longer has the power to condemn us.

Day 15

GO OUT AND PLAY

by Steve Brown

I desire mercy, and not sacrifice.

Matthew 12:7

Do not let anyone take away from you the reality that, because of Jesus Christ, "It is finished."

Justin Holcomb is a friend and former student of mine. He got his PhD from Emory University; he's a brilliant young man. Justin is an ordained Anglican minister and now works for my ministry, Key Life Network. Most importantly, he loves Jesus with all his heart, and he's even written a really wonderful book called *On the Grace of God.*[2] He gets this grace stuff really well. One time I asked him, "Justin, how did you start knowing about grace?"

"My father taught me," he said. "I was just a little kid, maybe seven. Our neighbors were going to move, and I didn't want them to. So I snuck into their house and stopped up all their drains and turned on the water and flooded the house."

I said, "At seven?"

"Oh yeah. It did thousands of dollars' worth of damage. And when I realized what I'd done, I was so ashamed. But I lied. I said, 'How could anybody do something like that, Dad?' And my dad said, 'I don't know how somebody could be that destructive.'

"For a whole week all I did was pray. I prayed that God wouldn't let me be caught. And I asked for forgiveness over and over and over again. One afternoon about a week later, my dad said, 'Son, did you have anything to do with the flooding of our neighbor's house?'"

When Justin lied through his teeth, his father said, "Son, the neighbor told me he saw you go in and do it." Justin began to weep, and his father went on. "I'm not just angry about what you did. I'm angry because you lied to me. You need to get straight with God and you need to get straight with me, and you're going to have everything you like removed until Jesus returns."

Justin said, "Daddy, every night I've asked God to forgive me."

"You asked God to forgive you?"

"Yes."

"Oh. That's different. Well, you're forgiven. Go on out and play."

Justin said the first time he ever talked about Jesus to his friends was when he told them what had happened.

Thought to Remember for Today

The only people who are able to extend forgiveness to sinners are those who have drunk deeply of the forgiveness that has been extended to them. Today, as you consider how Justin's father handled his sin, ask the Lord to help you believe you are forgiven and know you are free to "go out and play."

SEATED WITH HIM

by Bryan Chappell

*If then you have been raised with Christ, seek the things that
are above, where Christ is, seated at the right hand of God.*

Colossians 3:1

As you study Paul's words in Colossians 3:1, as he identified the status we have by the grace of God, notice there's a mystery in that first phrase: "If then you have been raised with Christ." That's resurrection language, isn't it? "If you've been resurrected." Now, he was talking to living people as though they had already died. How could he be talking to living people as if they had already died?

The answer is in Colossians 2:12, where the apostle described Christians as those "having been buried with him in baptism, in which you were also raised with him through faith in the powerful working of God, who raised him from the dead."

I must tell you, it is not normal in our day and age to think of a baptism as a death certificate, but that's exactly what it is. If you were a first-century Jew, or even a first-century Gentile coming out of pagan religion, this is what your baptism meant: all that has been true of you—your religion, your associations, your lifestyle, your family—is now no longer where you're finding your identity. They are, in a way, dead to you. And you are dead to them. You've been brought into real life under the true God, whose name is Jesus.

A year ago in Morocco, a young man came out of a church and was set upon by numerous people who tried to murder him. Rescued by the Christians in the church, he subsequently came to the United States and discovered his very own family had ordered his murder. "You are dead to us," they said. But he was alive now to a new existence in Christ.

The apostle was making much of that when he said in Colossians 3:1, "If then you have been raised with Christ"—in this new life—"seek the things that are above, where Christ is, seated at the right hand of God." Now, each word is important to understand the greatness of the grace of God. Jesus is raised to God in heaven, no longer dead.

If you are identified with Him, if you are united to Him and He is "seated at the right hand of God," where are you? Seated at the right hand of God.

Thought to Remember for Today

Your baptism signifies that you have died and have been raised again with a completely new identity, citizenship, and place of residence. What was once true about you is no longer true. By God's grace you have been raised up to sit at the place of honor with Christ.

HIDDEN WITH CHRIST

by Bryan Chappell

Set your minds on things that are above…. For you have died, and your life is hidden with Christ in God. When Christ who is your life appears, then you also will appear with him in glory.

Colossians 3:2–4

Paul told us we should "set [our] minds on things that are above." Why? "For you have died, and your life is hidden with Christ in God." Now, you understand that Jesus is united to God. And if you're united to Jesus and He's united to God, then you're with Christ in God. He says "hidden with Christ in God."

Do you know why you're hidden? The answer is in verse 4: "When Christ who is your life appears …" Christ is your life. But verses 2 and 3 say you're dead. Now verse 4 says Christ is your life. So I've got a question for you: If you're dead, and Jesus is your life, who are you?

Well, of course, nobody wants to say he or she is Jesus! And that's a good thing. So I'll change the way I ask the question. If you're dead and Jesus is your life, whose identity do you have? You have the identity of Christ. It's as though your identity has been obscured by His. You're with Him. This means what's true of Him—God's love for Him, His righteousness before the Father, His position of favor in the heavens—is true of you, because you're dead and His life is in your place because you're united to Him.

Sometimes at dinner my daughter and I play a game we call "Napkin War." When we're done eating I wait until she pretends to look away, wad up my napkin, and throw it at her. And as soon as I hit her, she'll pick up that napkin or wad up her own napkin and come right back at me. Suddenly the war is on. But I always win because I'm a better shot. So my daughter has discovered an ingenious way to protect herself. She gets up out of her chair and hides behind her mother. She knows I won't throw my napkin at her mother! She's hidden—she's safe—from all I could throw at her. Think about that, and apply it to your relationship with the Father through Christ.

Thought to Remember for Today

You and I, before a holy and just God, are rightly deserving of the wrath of hell itself. But by the grace of God, we are united to Christ, and with Him we are hidden from the wrath of

God. You are in the place of privilege and rest and love because of the grace of God on your behalf. Won't you let yourself rest in that beautiful truth today?

WITH HIM IN GLORY

by Bryan Chappell

When Christ who is your life appears, then
you also will appear with him in glory.

Colossians 3:4

These major aspects of the grace of God—that we are dead and raised with Christ and that we are hidden with Christ in God—are already established, already true, and are stated in the past tense. The reality is already here, but even that is not the fullness of the grace of God. He's not just going to look at what's past or present; He's going to look to the future as well.

"Then you also *will* appear with him in glory" (emphasis added). I must tell you, I don't exactly know all that this entails. When Christ returns to claim this world as the Sovereign King of the Universe, when He comes again in all His glory, then you and I will appear with Him in glory. So when His glory appears, that glory gets to be shared. Even the apostles did not fully understand what that meant. John said, "What we will be has not yet appeared; but we know that when he appears we shall be like him, because we shall see him as he is" (1 John 3:2).

In his amazing book *The Weight of Glory*, C. S. Lewis described it for us this way: "Remember that the dullest and most uninteresting person you can talk to may one day be a creature which if you saw it now, you would strongly be tempted to worship."[3] Why? Because the radiance of the glory of God will be theirs in Christ Jesus.

Now, you and I know ourselves, our weaknesses, our sins, our frailties, and our disappointments. We're well acquainted with the longing we have to be with Jesus, which never seems like it will be fulfilled because we are way off the mark so often.

But God knows all this and still says, "But you're raised with Christ and seated with Him at the right hand of God." When Jesus appears, you and I will have the glory of the Son of God, who created the world and the universe in which you and I live. That is how great the grace of God is.

Thought to Remember for Today

While it is true that we live in the here and now, the Holy Spirit has spoken great hope to us through these words from Paul: "You also will appear with him in glory" (Col. 3:4). We don't know exactly what that means, but we do know we will be completely changed, will have put off this old shell and put on a new life that, as Lewis penned, if we could see it now, we would fall down in worship. Today you're on a trajectory that will unavoidably end in your complete transformation.

REMEMBER WHO YOU ARE

by Bryan Chappell

*If then you have been raised with Christ,
seek the things that are above.*

Colossians 3:1

Once again we return to Colossians 3, and this time we ask, "Does grace lead to godliness?" I mean, if God's going to forgive you anyway, if His mercy is infinite, if His love is unconditional, if it's all grace, why be good at all? Just bank on all that grace.

There is a math of the mind that clearly can take advantage of the grace of God to say, "It doesn't matter. I'll just do as I please, and He'll make it right later." And believe it or not, that theology *is* somewhat undeniable because His grace is infinite, and He will forgive repeatedly, and His mercy is far beyond your worst sin. But the reason grace is powerful for godliness is because there is a *chemistry of the heart* that is greater than the math of the mind.

In these verses the apostle is going to do something with that great statement about who you are and how that should affect the chemistry of your heart. Now, he's going to say what's expected of those who are raised with Christ, hidden from His wrath, and due to appear with His glory. When he said, "If then you have been raised with Christ, seek the things that are above," he was saying, "Just consider this; think on these things: You've been separated from the evil of the earth. You've been separated from that which is polluting. Think about where you really are and act accordingly."

A Hurricane Katrina survivor related how he and his family fled to their attic as water quickly rose and flooded the first and second floors of their house. As the water continued to rise, they realized they were going to drown, and so they kicked out their roof and were rescued. As the man shared his story, he began to shake with the reality that they had been facing death, but were given life again.

Thought to Remember for Today

Paul said to you and to me in words we have trouble seeing for all their weight, "I want you to set your mind on this. I want this to grip you. I want this reality to be what you are living day in and day out. Do you remember what you were and what you deserve but where grace has brought you now? You set your mind on this."

IDENTITY MANAGEMENT
by David Zahl

*There is neither Jew nor Greek, there is neither slave nor free,
there is no male and female, for you are all one in Christ Jesus.*
Galatians 3:28

Identity is simply anything we use to justify our existence. And it's a matter, therefore, of both distinction and indistinction—meaning, we want to stand out in our identity, but we want to stand out in order to *blend in.* So we have this conflict going on within us—something you see playing out constantly on social media—in which we want to be seen as uniquely us but to be accepted by others and brought in closer to be a part of the crowd.

Now, the same generation that invented the big, dysfunctional parade of social media is the one that grew up under the pop-cultural therapists like Oprah Winfrey, in a culture of extreme validation. This generation didn't just graduate from high school to college, but from kindergarten to first grade. It reminds me of that scene in *The Incredibles,* where the father doesn't feel like going to his son's fourth-grade graduation, complaining, "He's just going into the fifth grade. It's not a graduation."

We think we have to stand out to blend in. But now the corollary has sunk into our DNA, deepening the conflict in us by reminding us that "when everybody is special, no one is." We are longing for connection, but we are also afraid of intimacy. The beauty of Facebook, and the source of its power, is that it enables us to be social while sparing us the inconvenience of actually showing up and the embarrassment of really being known. In this sense you might say social media is a vehicle of control. And what does the doctrine of original sin say about us if not that we are people who are addicted to control? We especially want to control what others think of us. We want to manage our images, our identities. We want to be our own PR directors.

Now think about Galatians 3:28. "There is neither Jew nor Greek, there is neither slave nor free, there is no male and female." That is a deconstruction of identity, if there ever was one.

But what's this got to do with grace? Well, our attempts at managing our identity are really about justification. Self-justification is at the core of our very souls. So it's no coincidence that the gospel of grace addresses this head-on and establishes the Christian's identity outside of him- or herself and inside of Jesus Christ.

Thought to Remember for Today

We tend to believe our achievements are not something we do but *who we are*. So when achievement is taken away or simply gets threatened, we go bananas. This is one of the reasons we all need the beautiful, saving word that we are justified by faith in Christ.

JESUS LOVES THE REAL YOU

by David Zahl

There is neither Jew nor Greek, there is neither slave nor free, there is no male and female, for you are all one in Christ Jesus.

Galatians 3:28

Now, if what the Bible says is true about original sin—that all have fallen short of the glory of God, that we have inherited the sin of Adam, which says, "I don't really want God to be in control; I want to be in control; I'm going to be my own god"—it's natural that social media would consume our daily lives. Through it we can be the mediators of our own value and worth.

Thomas Cranmer once said, "What the heart loves, the will chooses and then the mind justifies."[4] We're not rational beings, in other words. The mind doesn't direct the will; the mind is actually captive to what the will wants. And the will is in turn captive to what the heart wants.

Basically, we are self-justification machines. We think we make our decisions because we've weighed our reasons and chosen logically, but in fact, we just do what we want. And then afterward we go back and invent a reason, a justification, for it. (If you don't believe you do this, just ask your spouse.)

But even those for whom online identity construction is not an active pursuit, we still edit by omission, don't we? Think about your online life: the difference between your status updates and your browser history. I'm not just talking about pornography, by the way, though I am talking about that, too. Our browser histories are such an incredible picture of the human condition. Because in one window, maybe you're crafting some beautiful document—maybe about your faith, maybe a loving letter to a friend. But in the next window, you're googling your ex-boyfriend. In the next window, you're trying to figure out how to spell a word you don't know how to spell. In the next, you're searching WebMD for the disease you think you might have. And in the next, you're clicking on some link to the latest celebrity gossip.

Your browser history tells the truth about you. Your status updates tell *part* of the truth about you. And this gap between who you think you should be or who you'd like to be and who you *actually are*, that's your need for a Savior.

Thought to Remember for Today

Remember the modern proverb, "The real you is the you that you are when nobody is looking." But remind yourself in God's grace that Jesus Christ loves *that* you. He doesn't love an image of you or a version of you. He died and rose again for the "browser history" you. Jesus loves the real you.

THE DECONSTRUCTION OF IDENTITY

by David Zahl

There is neither Jew nor Greek, there is neither slave nor free, there is no male and female, for you are all one in Christ Jesus.

Galatians 3:28

We do not engage with God according to what we can bring to the table. Our real relationships with God begin when we are exposed, when the law does its deconstructing work. And our fabricated identities need to die! The purpose of the law is to bring people to their knees, looking to the One who has justified them already.

Football coach Urban Meyer tells about how his father pressured him to compete. At a time when Urban knew he didn't have the skill to continue in baseball, he told his dad he was quitting. His father informed him that if he quit, he would no longer be welcome in their home. As an adult, Urban embraced that performance-related mind-set of his father, going on to win back-to-back national championships as the coach for the Florida

Gators. But these victories were short-lived because every time they won, the screws just got tighter and tighter. So much so that anything but perfection was viewed as failure. Then Urban started to have worsening chest pains. And a few hours after the Gators finally lost in 2009, he was found on the floor of his house, unable to move. He'd finally come to his breaking point.

At one point after his breakdown, Urban went to see his father, who was in the hospital. There was a report on the television about the possibility of Urban taking a job at Ohio State, and his father said, "Hey, you gonna do that?"

"I don't know," Urban said. "What do you think?"

"Nah," his dad responded. "I don't care who wins or loses." Never before had Urban asked his dad for an opinion and not gotten blunt advice. In fact, in his father's answer there was a measure of absolution.

Three days after his father's funeral, Urban accepted the job at Ohio State. But this time his approach was entirely different. Instead of signing a contract with the school, he signed a contract with his family—that he wouldn't be missing any more of his kids' games and he wouldn't be working more than sixty hours a week. It was a contract of love, and born out of tremendous deconstruction of identity. He was a new man.[5]

Thought to Remember for Today

Christ is our Mediator. In Christ our hope is found. This simply means we are judged not according to our wins or losses, but on the basis of Christ's action and identity.

Day 23

THE IDENTITY GIFT

by David Zahl

*Not having a righteousness of my own that comes from
the law, but that which comes through faith in Christ,
the righteousness from God that depends on faith.*

Philippians 3:9

Through the death and resurrection of Jesus Christ, His identity
and righteousness have been reckoned to us when received by
faith. What did Jesus do on the cross? He emptied Himself of all
identity. Isn't that what Philippians says? And as the Augsburg
Confession puts it, "Christ's merits are given to us so that we
might be reckoned righteous by our trust in the merits of Christ,
when we believe in Him, as though we had merits of our own."[6]

In other words, identity is a gift. It's not to be earned; it is
bestowed. It is given by God, not the court of public opinion, not
even the court of condemnation inside our own minds.

In the gospel we don't get instructions about how to create a
better version of ourselves. We get a new identity, a gift. It's a matter of being, not doing. It's a matter of giving up on the idea of

who you think you need to be and finding out that what remains is the real you, loved and accepted by God on account of Christ.

So Christianity explodes the idea of ever reaching peace through personal achievement. You will never be cool enough, good-looking enough, wealthy enough. Christianity reestablishes the proper basis for self-understanding. W. H. Auden, the great English poet, wrote, "The blessed will not care what angle they are regarded from, having nothing to hide."[7] Christ brings the end of double lives, the end of hiding.

If the fruit of the law is narcissism, loneliness, and anxiety, the fruit of the gospel is honesty, and honesty works itself out in repentance and confession. Because we are forgiven, we are free to finally talk about what's really going on in our lives, independent of the judgments that might provoke. In repentance, God meets us in our weakness, not in our strength.

Thought to Remember for Today

God has done for us what we could not do for ourselves. He nailed our narcissistic instincts to a cross. And rising again, He established a new identity for each of us. The starting point is grace—not works, not public opinion. And this is a life of freedom, where we can own up to our shortcomings, independent of judgments.

A KINGDOM FOR THE WEAK

by Ray Ortlund

For theirs is the kingdom of heaven.

Matthew 5:3

Jesus welcomes into His kingdom only the people who have defied Him and offended Him and sinned so badly that their own righteousness is gone for good. They've lost their innocence, and now they've come to Him with nothing but need. They don't admire themselves anymore. They mourn over themselves. But Jesus is happy with them, and He wants them to know He's happy with them. He's happy with you, to the praise of the glory of His grace.

So the Beatitudes are not just another passage in the Bible. The Beatitudes summarize what real Christianity looks like. The Beatitudes portray what repentance looks like, the way repentance thinks, the way repentance feels.

The kingdom of Jesus is for sinners and penitents, and for them only. It's for people who have failed so badly they have no bargaining chips left, and they refuse to fake it. They bring their need to God; He gives them Jesus; and He creates with these unlikely people something new in this world that will last forever: His kingdom.

And the Beatitudes are not a menu to choose from. They're a coherent whole, so it's all or nothing. When Jesus preached this sermon on the Galilean hillside and all those people were out there, He didn't look at one group and say, "Oh, nice to see the poor in spirit here today. And then the mourners over there— glad you guys could get out of bed. And way in the back are the meek. You know, they'll never push themselves up to the front row, and …" The poor in spirit, the mourners, the meek, and all the rest are *the same people* viewed from different angles of vision.

How do we know that? The first and last Beatitudes, found in verses 3 and 10 in Matthew 5, both say, "For theirs is the kingdom of heaven." So those two matching declarations wrap around all the Beatitudes, showing they belong together as a unit. Here's why that matters: for me, meekness is not easy, but mourning isn't that hard; so I would treat these verses as a menu of preferences, and I would gravitate toward what I perceive to be my strengths. But Jesus means every word here for every single one of us. So we want to move toward our weaknesses, because that's where our King is waiting for us with grace.

Thought to Remember for Today

Contrary to popular thought, the kingdom of heaven is not populated by the strong, the sinless, the consistently victorious. It is populated by those who know they are poor and weak and naked. It is populated by those who have put down their weapons of self-justification and rest in Christ's promised love alone.

THE BLESSED IMPOVERISHED

by Ray Ortlund

Blessed are the poor in spirit.

Matthew 5:3

Let us keep reflecting on this important verse, asking again, "Who are the poor in spirit?" Now, Jesus is implying that all the people who think they've earned His attention are in fact excluded and on their way to hell. And as evidence of that, they tend to create hell on earth while they live. Jesus is telling all the people who think they're important that they don't count. He's telling all the people who think they're smart that they flunk. He's telling all the sinners and whores and porn addicts and hypocrites and failures and idiots and weaklings who turn to Him that the future of the world is theirs.

The Pharisees looked at those very people and said, "You're the ones who are bringing society down. You're the problem." Jesus looked at the same people turning to Him, and He said, "You're the ones I'm going to build My kingdom with."

To be poor in spirit ... What does that mean? It doesn't mean a dull personality; Jesus gives us sparkle. Spirit-filled human beings are a riot to be with. They are just a blast. They're human; they're free. But Jesus is saying wealth begins with poverty, life begins with death, a better future begins with facing the past. When He talks about the poor, He doesn't mean people who have only a little. He means people who have *nothing*.

The poor in spirit are sinners who have squandered their chance in life, but in their desperation they turn to Jesus. The poor in spirit look at the cross. They see the Son of God dying for their bungled lives, and they know they can't put in a claim on God. The old spirit of demands died when the Lord taught us to pray, "Forgive us our debts." The poor in spirit feel that indebtedness. Jesus is saying, "Do you realize God owes you nothing? Perfect! You're the ones He's going to bless."

Thought to Remember for Today

When we want to start a new project, we recruit the cool people and the winners and the heavy hitters and the people who are smart and funny and impressive. But Jesus looks for the losers who are down so low they need everything. I mean, who would start a religion with sinners? Jesus, that's who.

OUR BEST WORKS NEED CLEANSING

by Ray Ortlund

Blessed are the poor in spirit.

Matthew 5:3

Here we are again. I don't think we can ponder this blessing too much. Sadly, not all churches are in this blessed state of impoverishment. Jesus said to His church in Laodicea, "You say, I am rich, I have prospered, and I need nothing, not realizing that you are wretched, pitiable, poor, blind, and naked" (Rev. 3:17). I mean, think about that. You're walking down the street, and here comes a guy. You see him down about half a block away. *Whoa.* He is wretched, pitiable, poor, blind, and naked—and kind of banged up because he's walked into telephone poles and mailboxes and stuff. And you walk up to him and you say, "Sir, may I help you?" And he says, "I am rich. I have prospered. I need nothing." He's crazy.

And when that spirit enters into a church, it stifles the creation of a gospel culture. All the Laodicean church could think about

was its strengths. What it needed was honesty about its weaknesses, because it is weakness—and *guilty* weakness—brought to
Jesus that brings the blessings down.

During the first Great Awakening, George Whitefield, the
Anglican evangelist said:

> If you want to have peace with God you must
> be troubled for the sins of your best duties
> and performances. You must be brought to
> see that God may damn you for the best
> prayer you ever put up. Our best duties are
> so many splendid sins. Self-righteousness is
> the last idol taken out of the heart.[8]

So we need the gospel to tell us the truth. What is that truth?
William Beveridge put it this way:

> I cannot pray but I sin. I cannot hear or
> preach a sermon but I sin. I cannot give alms
> or receive the sacrament but I sin. I can't so
> much as confess my sins but my confessions
> are further aggravations of them. My repen-
> tance needs to be repented of. My tears need

washing. And the very washing of my tears
needs still to be washed over again with the
blood of my Redeemer.[9]

That's being poor in spirit.

Thought to Remember for Today

These are the people Jesus identifies with—those who are as sinful
as everyone else, but they own it, they fess up, and they trust only
in Jesus. These will experience the kingdom of heaven and their
churches will feel like heaven on earth.

GRACE FOR YOUR INABILITY

by Elyse Fitzpatrick

You shall love the Lord your God.

Matthew 22:37

Before I can give you the really good news, you know what I need to do? I must give you the bad news. Here's what God's law says: "You are to love the Lord your God with your whole soul, mind, and strength. You are to love the Lord your God with everything that is within you, 24 hours a day, 7 days a week, 365 days a year."

How are you doing with that? While we're at it, let's not forget to add on top of that, "You are to love your neighbor the way you already love yourself."

Now, let's take that law and apply it to the family home. Consider these verses from Ephesians 5–6, which tell us how the Great Commandment is supposed to play out in your house: "Wives, submit to your own husbands, as to the Lord.... Let the wife see that she respects her husband.... Husbands, love your wives, as Christ loved the church and gave himself up for her.... Do not be harsh with [her].... Children, obey your parents in the Lord, for this is right.... Fathers [Parents], do not provoke your children to anger, but bring them up in the discipline and instruction of the Lord."

Okay, here's my problem: I *want* to do all those things required of me. I hear those verses, and I say, "Yes, Lord. Make that true of me. I want that to be me." But I continually fail. I get up in the morning, and I pray that God will help me to love my neighbor. And then at the end of the day, I realize that even though I may be growing, my progress is painfully slow. And sometimes I see no progress at all.

Does God really mean I have to love my neighbor? Does He really mean I have to lay down my life for my neighbor? Does He really mean I'm supposed to submit to my husband? What, are you kidding?

I find myself echoing Paul's thoughts from Romans 7, "So I find it to be a law that when I want to do right, evil lies close at hand" (v. 21). I want to say, like Paul says, "I delight in the law of God, in my inner being" (v. 22). I do. But "I see in my members another law waging war against the law of my mind and making me captive to the law of sin that dwells in my members" (v. 23).

Who will deliver me?

Thought to Remember for Today

And it is there, in that place—and only in that place—that we find grace. There's no other place to find it. The only place you can find grace is when you say, "Nothing in my hands I bring. Simply to Thy Cross I cling."[10] I throw myself on the mercy of God, and that's the only place grace resides.

Day 28

GOD HAS DONE WHAT THE LAW COULD NEVER DO

by Elyse Fitzpatrick

For the law of the Spirit of life has set you free in
Christ Jesus from the law of sin and death.

Romans 8:2

How did Paul answer his "Who will deliver me?" question in Romans 7:24? In verse 25, he said, "Thanks be to God through Jesus Christ our Lord!" Jesus is the One who delivers us from bondage to sin. I wish there were no chapter break between Romans 7 and Romans 8, because Paul went right on and said, "There is therefore now no condemnation for those who are in Christ Jesus" (Rom. 8:1).

No condemnation. I don't care what you did this morning. I don't care what's going on in your mind right now. You may be sitting next to somebody you really wish weren't your neighbor. There is therefore *right now* no condemnation.

The reality is that I deserve condemnation. And so do you. But when we put our trust in Jesus Christ, we are united to Him by our faith and His position becomes our position. "There is therefore now no condemnation *for those who are in Christ Jesus.*" There is no condemnation for us, because we are in Christ and there is no condemnation left for Him!

There is a righteous requirement of the law, and you're supposed to fulfill it. But did you? No! Somebody had to fulfill it for you. And He did! "The righteous requirement of the law might be fulfilled in us, who walk not according to the flesh"—what we were just confessing—"but according to the Spirit" (Rom. 8:4).

How can there be no condemnation? Listen, if God's law cannot be violated, and He doesn't lessen it, and He isn't kidding, and if transgression of the law brings death, how can there be no condemnation? How can it be that the righteous requirement of the law has already been fulfilled in me? Because God has done something the law could never do. He sent "his own Son in the likeness of sinful flesh and for sin" (Rom. 8:3). The Incarnate Son, Jesus, was sent as a sacrifice for our sin, by paying the penalty for all our sin, by dying on the cross in our place.

Thought to Remember for Today

Here's good news: Jesus Christ has already paid the penalty for your sin by dying on the cross. He took that cup of the righteous anger of God's wrath, and He drank it down to its dregs for you "so that the righteous requirement of the law might be fulfilled" in you, and all the penalty you owe for every single unkind word, every single selfish thought, has been paid by Him on the cross in your place.

GOOD NEWS FOR YOUR FAMILY

by Elyse Fitzpatrick

That the righteous requirement of the
law might be fulfilled in us.

Romans 8:4

There is no condemnation for us because Jesus Himself perfectly fulfilled all the law in our place, including the laws about relationships and family. Jesus perfectly fulfilled, in His incarnation and in His sinless life, all of God's rules for family life. Jesus lived a whole and perfect life for you.

So now we come back to our law. We read things like, "Wives, submit to your husbands as to the Lord" and "Let the wife see that she respects her husband." At Gethsemane, Jesus perfectly submitted to His Father's will. Think about it, women. Do you think submission is hard for you? He, the second Person of the Trinity, was writhing on the ground underneath the will of His Father, to which He submitted and said, "Not my will, but thine, be done" (Luke 22:42 KJV). Jesus understands all about the difficulties of submission.

Jesus knows what it's like to love, even when it's extremely difficult. The law says husbands are to "love [their] wives, as Christ loved the church and gave himself up for her" (Eph. 5:25) and they are not to be harsh with their wives (Col. 3:19). Jesus perfectly loved His bride, the church. From eternity past, before she was ever on the scene—before there was a scene!—He loved her. The Father gave her to the Son, and the Son said, "Yes, I will love her, and I will lay down My life for her."

"Children, obey your parents in the Lord" (Eph. 6:1). Jesus is the righteous Son who obeyed His Father's will and submitted to His mother and father, even when they were in the wrong. Luke tells us He submitted to them.

"Fathers, do not provoke your children to anger, but bring them up in the discipline and instruction of the Lord" (Eph. 6:4). Jesus was a good father figure to His siblings and supported and cared for them for however many years He spent as the head of their home. He never once provoked them. He brought them up in the discipline and instruction of the Lord.

Jesus has fulfilled all of the law for you in your place, if you believe. He's taken all the punishment you deserve for all the ways you've blown it in your family. He's taken all of the punishment you deserve, and He bore it for you. He is your righteousness.

Thought to Remember for Today

If you believe these words are true, then here is what's true of you: His record is yours. Wives, you are forgiven, and your record is one of perfect submission and respect. Husbands, you are forgiven, and your record is one of humble love and self-sacrifice. Children, you are forgiven, and your record is one of perfect obedience.

Day 30

YOU ALREADY HAVE EVERYTHING YOU NEED

by Elyse Fitzpatrick

Christ ... is your life.

Colossians 3:4

In Christ you have everything you need, and because of that, wives, you're free to respect and submit to your husband because you have a heavenly husband who has loved you and will care for your soul and give you all you need. You don't need to fight for your own way. You can trust Jesus because He knows all about submission to ungodly authority. You don't have to worry anymore about whether or not you're loved. Jesus loves you and has chosen you. You are His beloved bride. You have a new identity.

Husbands, you are free now to love your wives generously, freely, joyfully, and sacrificially, because your Savior has loved you, and you don't need to demand respect or submission or anything else. He's given you everything you need. You no longer need to fight for what is rightfully yours or demand submission in the kitchen or in the bedroom. You don't have to neglect your family to worship at the altars of the NFL or the NBA or the MLB or anything else on your television. You can lay down your life for your wife because Jesus is with you, and He knows by experience what loving a sinner is like. What she thinks of you is not your identity. Whether or not she desires you is not your identity. Christ is your life.

Children, you are free now to submit to the authority over you. Jesus knows by experience what submission to authority is like. He submitted to His heavenly Father, and He submitted to His earthly mother and father, and Jesus will give you all the love and respect you truly need. Children, you are forgiven and you are righteous.

Parents, you're free to love your children and train them in the gospel because Jesus knows what it's like to love little sinners, and He will sustain you. You no longer have to worry about being the perfect parent because you are a forgiven parent. You are forgiven for all the times you discouraged your children or provoked them to anger. You are loved. Christ is your life.

Can you see? Everything you need is in Christ. He is your identity. You are God's chosen ones, holy and beloved. And as the Lord has loved and forgiven you, so also now you are free to love and forgive.

Thought to Remember for Today

Even though your heart may be resonating with these truths, you're going to have to come back here over and over again, because the opportunities to get angry and judge or to love and forgive come to us over and over again. So turn to grace every day, over and over again. Remember, you have His identity.

WE ARE THE CALLED

by Matt Chandler

*And we know that for those who love God all things
work together for good, for those who are called according
to his purpose. For those whom he foreknew he also
predestined to be conformed to the image of his Son, in
order that he might be the firstborn among many brothers.
And those whom he predestined he also called.*

Romans 8:28–30

What is the basis for our relationship with God? How does our relationship with God *work*?

Our answer begins with a look at Romans 8:28–30. In particular, let's consider the words "those who are called." I think, for the sake of vibrancy in regard to our relationship with God, we have to keep ever before us that He *called* us.

I played basketball and football when I was kid, just like my son does (and I was terrible at both, just like my son is). And after I started playing high school football—and by "playing" I mean they let me be on the team—a guy named Jeff Faircloth came up to me in the locker room and said, "Hey, I need to tell you about Jesus. When do you want to do that? You tell me when we're doing it, but it's happening."

Now, Jeff's version of Christianity was very different from the one I saw at home. But I found it compelling. So I started going to church with him. But church, honestly, was just the kitschiest, goofiest thing I'd ever seen. There was so much stacked against my ever believing in this Jesus Jeff followed. At that time, I had no language for the effectual call of God, and so I'd get in Jeff's car as he drove me home after church and I'd mock the whole thing. I mean, "Did we really just spell the word *joy* with our bodies? Did they really just do a skit with puppets?" But then Jeff would ask me if I wanted to go back and I kept saying "Yeah." I thought it was dumb; I thought Jeff was wrong; but I couldn't stay away.

Thought to Remember for Today

I know, looking back, that God was calling me. He was wooing me, and it wasn't because I was trying to get better. It was while I was at my worst. It was while I was belittling His name, while I was mocking His bride. It was while we were sinners that Christ died for us, and it is while we are sinners that God calls us to Himself.

Day 32

THOSE WHOM HE CALLED HE ALSO JUSTIFIED

by Matt Chandler

We ourselves are Jews by birth and not Gentile sinners;
yet we know that a person is not justified by works
of the law but through faith in Jesus Christ.

Galatians 2:15–16

God called us. God came and got you. God found you, rescued you, and wooed you. He drew you to Himself for what purpose? For "those whom he called he also justified" (Rom. 8:30). So what is justification?

We, of all people on earth, should get the idea of justification, because it's a legal term, and our culture loves legality. For instance, how many CSI TV shows are there these days? Like, twenty-four? How many versions of *Law & Order*? And that's just television. We love the law. All you need to do is give us a story about lawyers, prosecution, or good detective work, and we get sucked in; because as a culture, we love the idea of justice. So we should already understand what justification really entails: to be pardoned. Justification is a banging of the gavel of the Sovereign King of Glory that says you've been *pardoned in full*.

And how are we justified? Not by works of the law, but by faith, because the apostle Paul reminded his readers that five hundred years before the Law was given, Abraham was *justified by faith*. You're not justified because you cleaned up your act. We're not people who have pulled ourselves up by our bootstraps. Our testimony of salvation is not one of moral improvement.

Paul was so passionate about this that he said the exact same thing in his next sentence: "So we also have believed in Christ Jesus, in order to be justified by faith in Christ and not by works of the law, because"—here it is again, third time—"by works of the law no one will be justified." He came at this from multiple angles in just two verses (Gal. 2:15–16). You're not going to be able to be justified by the law, the law will not justify you, and all of us have been justified by faith in Christ.

We've got to grasp that because of the life, death, and resurrection of the Son, the royal Judge has pardoned all of our sin—past, present, and future. There's no mistrial, no double jeopardy. Because of Jesus, you are justified forever.

Thought to Remember for Today

If you don't get justification, you will always run from God rather than toward Him. You avoid people you've sinned against, don't you? If you've sinned against someone or lied to someone, don't you avoid that person? It's the same with God. You're going to run from Him to try to clean yourself up. And we clean ourselves up a lot like my four-year-old cleans up after herself—basically just smearing stuff into the cracks. But you don't have to do that with God. He justifies sinners.

NO LONGER A JUDGE, NOW A HEAVENLY FATHER

by Matt Chandler

For you did not receive the spirit of slavery to fall back into fear, but you have received the Spirit of adoption as sons, by whom we cry, "Abba! Father!"

Romans 8:15

Here's what I've learned now after eleven years pastoring in an area pervaded by Christian culture: these people don't struggle a whole lot with justification. They sort of think, *Yeah, yeah, God forgives me. I know that.* Now, whether or not they really believe it is a whole different issue. What I'm finding is there's a ton of people who can verbally explain the gospel as though God is a just Judge who has pardoned their sin, but then what ends up happening is that they just determine to go trying to never sin again. What's happened? Really, they've never made the turn in their understanding from God as just Judge to heavenly Father.

Here's a bit of my wife Lauren's story:

I grew up in a Christian home, trying very much to be a good girl. When I was eight, my relationship with Jesus was very simple, where you just go to church and pray. But entering the preteen and early teen years, I was really trying to figure out who I was. And looking back, I see that I always desired to look like somebody who seemed to have it all together. And then, as I got into college and then met my husband, I tried really hard to measure up to my idea of godly adulthood, and I thought, *Okay, I've got to be a good enough wife and a good enough student,* and so on and so on. And I was falling miserably short. So the Lord graciously let me fail. He let me be weak, He let me be frustrated and experience dissatisfaction in everything. I finally knew something had to give. I couldn't live this way anymore. I had this obsession with my identity. And moving forward for me meant admitting that I was weak, admitting that I didn't have it all together, and admitting that something was

wrong with my heart. I have to admit, even
though I'm a pastor's wife, that I don't have it
all together. I need Jesus. I need His gospel. I
need His gospel that saved me to also trans-
form me and sustain me, because I'd started
kind of just trying to do it on my own.

Thought to Remember for Today

Lauren would say she knew God loved her and forgave her, but
then she walked out of that pardon to say, "Okay, now, let me
earn it." And she forgot to rest in the reality that God isn't simply
her just Judge but also her loving heavenly Father. And He's that
for you, too.

NO BETTER VERSION OF YOU

by Matt Chandler

*For you did not receive the spirit of slavery to fall
back into fear, but you have received the Spirit of
adoption as sons, by whom we cry, "Abba! Father!"*

Romans 8:15

Honestly, I don't struggle much with wondering if God forgives me, but I do still consistently have to preach the gospel to myself to believe that He likes me *right now*. Do you know what I mean? It's easy to believe He likes Matt Chandler ten years from now. After some sanctification, that dude is going to be legit. But the Matt Chandler of today? Sometimes I think God loves me and is just kind of patient with me. He's just sort of *tolerating* me until I grow up a little more. But there's certainly no delight in Him toward me. There is no gladness of heart over my being one of His adopted sons.

Romans 8:15–17 is going to help us a bit with this kind of thinking. When God called you and justified you, He called you out of one of four big traps of spiritual slavery.

First, you had bought into the lie that a better version of you was going to solve all your problems. A better version of you, a wealthier version, a more disciplined version, a more fit version— these are lies. Setting our hearts there is like running on a treadmill all the days of your life. Running and running and going nowhere.

Second, you got rescued out of the slavery of wanting other people to validate you. And few things are as life-sucking and soul-crushing as needing others to validate you.

Third, you got rescued from the lures of the world, from the lie that what you need is more of what you already have, even though that hasn't satisfied you.

And fourth, He rescued you from religion itself. And religion is a funny one, because it's trying to tip scales that don't even exist. Works-based religion is a mirage.

All of these attempts at becoming "a better you" are anti-gospel. I don't know why we try to pretend we're more than we are. Jesus didn't die for some better version of us; those people don't even exist. He died for us, as we are.

Thought to Remember for Today

I will buy into the lie that just a better version of me will solve some of what I'm feeling. But God loves the real me, and Jesus died for the real me—and the real you. And He has given us His Spirit to keep delivering us from these traps we keep falling into and back into the loving, forgiving arms of the Father.

OUR INHERITANCE

by Matt Chandler

The Spirit himself bears witness with our spirit that we
are children of God, and if children, then heirs—heirs of
God and fellow heirs with Christ, provided we suffer with
him in order that we may also be glorified with him.

Romans 8:16–17

Paul said the Spirit bears witness to our spirit. It is so hard for us to believe God loves us, delights in us, and cheers us on in Christ, but Paul said the Spirit testifies to us that we are children of God. There are two ways He does that, and they sort of merge into a single word. First, we have a desire for obedience to God (although it's imperfectly executed). And then there is a gladness of heart in the Lord (certainly of varying degrees at varying times). A desire for obedience plus gladness of heart. Together these form the simple word *pursuit*. We pursue God.

Now, what does that pursuit look like? Well, it's always going to involve the Word of God; it's always going to involve spending time with God in prayer. The rest may depend on your gifting and personality and circumstances.

But then Paul said we're "heirs of God and fellow heirs with Christ." We learn that you and I will reign with Jesus in a remade heaven and earth. Part of our inheritance is a resurrected body. Our bodies will one day be replaced with bodies that will not be broken down. Then, ultimately and best of all, we get God! If you got the new heaven and the new earth and you got your new body, but you didn't get God, then it wouldn't be worth it. The soul was created for Him. And the good news of the gospel is that because of Jesus Christ, we get God regardless of our circumstances.

But then Paul said we are heirs "provided we suffer with him." Anyone else wish that little sentence weren't in there?

Ed Welch once said we think sanctification looks like strength when it actually looks like weakness. Sanctification is not you with your chest puffed out, a cape in the wind, having just memorized the book of Romans. No, it looks like you're tired, weary, and busted up. It's the mercy of God, in fact, to at times wound you like a surgeon would wound a patient who needs to live. Don't despise the difficult days. God is at work in the mess. It's imperative that we keep our eyes on our inheritance.

Thought to Remember for Today

You know, it pleased the heart of God to save you. Today, ask the Lord to continue testifying to you by His Spirit that you are His, that you are deeply loved, forever pardoned, eternally justified, and gloriously promised a great inheritance.

Day 36

THE POWER OF THE GOSPEL
by J.D. Greear

We love because he first loved us.
1 John 4:19

In Genesis 3 we find that sin has left us spiritually dead, meaning that the heart of our love for and delight in God was killed. Our original sin was idolatry. We valued what the Tree of Knowledge of Good and Evil could give us more than we valued God.

St. Augustine said Adam was choosing the company of his wife more than he was choosing God. He put more weight on being with Eve than he did on actually knowing and walking with God. In effect, he worshipped that way of living more than God.

God's response was to give us over to our idols. Our hearts became, as John Calvin said, idol factories.[11] Because of our idolatry, God's laws to love and to serve and to glorify Him became unnatural to us. And when we do try to keep them, we chafe against them.

Imagine I have a metal bar that I am going to try to bend right in front of you. I take that metal bar, and I bend it and get it down to a certain shape. Then, one of two things happens. Either I stop applying pressure on the bar, at which point the bar immediately snaps back into its original shape. Or maybe I put so much pressure on it that it snaps in two. This is a picture of what happens to our hearts when we apply God's law without the gospel. We either give up trying when the external pressure is removed, or we break spiritually. The law can demand our conformity, but it is powerless to reshape our hearts.

Martin Luther said this was the dilemma of the Great Commandment.[12] If you love someone, you don't need to be *commanded* to love them. You just *love them*! Luther concluded that what the law actually requires is freedom from the law, because if you really love God, you won't need to be commanded. You *couldn't* be commanded. You would just do it.

Thought to Remember for Today

For works to be good in God's sight, they cannot be a means to anything else. They must come from the inward fount of the new man. Just as lovers do not need to be told what to do and say, a truly righteous heart needs no commands to be righteous. I never need to be commanded to kiss my wife, to eat a steak, or take a nap. Those things just come from the inward fount of who I am. Because you believe God has first loved you, your love for Him will flow more and more naturally. You will love, not because you're commanded to love but because you are loved.

GOOD WORKS DONE FOR US
by J.D. Greear

We love because he first loved us.
1 John 4:19

Genesis 3 shows us the source of spiritual death. But one of the other effects of the fall is that we also realize our spiritual nakedness. We were naked, of course, before we sinned. But as Athanasius used to explain, our nakedness did not bother us then because we were clothed in the love and acceptance of God. When we sinned, that acceptance was stripped away, and we felt our nakedness.

What do human beings do when they sense nakedness? If you have a problem sleepwalking and you wake up at two o'clock in the morning in a 24-hour Walmart, standing there stark naked, what's your first impulse? You probably won't think, "Now that I'm here, I might as well get some paper towels." No, you think, "Holy cow, I'm naked!" You try to hide. That's the condition men and women live in. Something's been exposed. We feel vulnerable, ashamed in some way. And like we've got to do something to clothe ourselves.

Luther explained that one of the primary ways we choose to fix that problem is by good works. The problem is that when our good works are done for self-justification, as a way really to "cover ourselves," then they're not really that good. They're just another means of serving ourselves.

Charles Spurgeon illustrated this concept with a story about a king. One day a poor subject of his showed up with a huge carrot. He said, "Oh King, I've loved you for years. And when I saw this carrot grow in my garden, I *knew* this was a carrot fit for the glory of the king." The king was genuinely touched, and said, "Sir, I care about you and I happen to own the farm right by yours, so I'm going to give you all that property because I am so moved by your gesture." Well, one of the king's shrewd courtiers thought, *If that's what the king would give for a carrot, imagine what he would do for a real gift!* So this court official came in the next day and said, "Oh King, you're the most awesome king ever. I really wanted to show you how much I love you as a king, so I brought you my magnificent horse, the finest horse in our country." The king, who was wise, saw through the courtier's gift and said, "Thank you." When the courtier questioned why he didn't get a gift in return, the king said, "Yesterday that servant was giving the carrot to me. Today you are giving that horse to *yourself.*"[13]

Thought to Remember for Today

God doesn't want the kind of obedience that's used as leverage. You can't bribe Him. He's after a whole new kind of obedience, the obedience that grows from desire, when you do righteousness because you love righteousness. The more you soak yourself in the good news of the gospel, the more you will delight in good deeds simply because you love the Lord.

ALIEN RIGHTEOUSNESS

by J.D. Greear

For God, who said, "Let light shine out of darkness,"
has shone in our hearts to give the light of the knowledge
of the glory of God in the face of Jesus Christ.

2 Corinthians 4:6

In contrast to the law, the apostle Paul said the gospel presents a righteousness and a power that is from God, what we might call an "alien" or "gift" righteousness.

The gospel reveals to us a God who is better than our idols, so it *re-wins* our hearts back to God. Paul said in 2 Corinthians 3:18, "We all … beholding the glory of the Lord, are being transformed." How is it that we are transformed from people who are idolaters to people who seek God's glory? Not by doing, but by *seeing—seeing* God's glory. And we see that glory in the face of Jesus Christ.

Most of the sins I struggle with have a common root: I give glory to what other people think about me. So even though I'm not an overly angry person, when I *do* get angry, it almost always goes back to me losing face with somebody.

When I worry—and I tend to worry a lot—it's almost always a fear of the same thing. I have this irrational fear that one day I'm going to show up to church and learn that everybody has simultaneously decided, "He's not that good; we're going to go somewhere else." I'll walk into a huge sanctuary, and it'll just be me, with my wife sitting on the front row. So I overwork. I cheat my family and the relationships that are close to me, because I'm afraid that if I'm not successful, I'm going to lose people's admiration.

When I lie it's always for one of two reasons. I tend to either exaggerate my accomplishments or minimize my weaknesses. Even here, I have the courage to tell you a few of my faults and be transparent, but deep down, a part of me is doing that so you'll admire me for my transparency!

The point is this: you can tell me all day long to stop being angry, to stop lying, and to stop worrying, but until you change what I give glory to, I'm still obeying or disobeying out of self-interest. And that's not going to last.

Thought to Remember for Today

Paul David Tripp said, "If we worshipped our way into sin, then the only way we can truly escape sin is to worship our way out." The Bible says the gospel changes what we worship by revealing to us a God who is better and more glorious than our idols, so that we become people who do righteousness because we crave righteousness, who seek God because we love God.

GRACE IS HEAVIER

by J.D. Greear

*For the grace of God has appeared, bringing salvation
for all people, training us to renounce ungodliness
and worldly passions, and to live self-controlled,
upright, and godly lives in the present age.*

Titus 2:11–12

What produces the ability to do all the things listed in Titus 2:11–12? The grace of God.

The problem is not that the power of sin is too strong. The problem is that your love for God is too weak. If your love for God grew, it would bring into captivity all of these things. How do our passions for God grow? Not by being told that they're supposed to grow, but by marveling at what God has done for us. The key in that verse is the word *appeared*. The grace of God has always been there, of course, but it has appeared to the heart of the hearer, because when God opens our eyes to behold the glory of God in the gospel, the passions of our hearts change so that we live godly, self-controlled lives.

So when I'm talking to the high school girl who just lost her virginity, I'm not telling her about the dangers of STDs or how much she's screwing up her chance at a happy marriage. I'm telling her there is a God who cares enough about her that He came to earth to pursue her, to die in her place for her sin, and that He loves her more than any dirtbag guy ever could. And if she would understand the love of the Father, which she's been seeking everywhere but in Him, then the seductions she faces in high school would not be nearly as strong over her.

When I'm dealing with the young man who is overwhelmed by pornography, I'm not just telling him how much he's messing up his heart and poisoning his future relationships. I am telling him that God created him to be a man of righteousness, that God shed His blood so he could become exactly that. Commands don't break the power of canceled sin; the acceptance God gives in Christ does. There is no way to believe and behold the gospel without also becoming more like Christ.

Grace is heavier than sin, and if we will lean into it, God's Spirit will help us live as those who are freed from the bondage of these lesser satisfactions, the ones that kill.

Thought to Remember for Today

Martyn Lloyd-Jones said the ultimate measure of our spirituality is our amazement at the grace of God. Growth in godliness is most fundamentally growth in our awareness of our need for grace. Christian growth this side of heaven is not getting to a point where you don't really feel like you need grace. Christian growth this side of heaven is becoming more intimately aware of how desperately you need it.

Day 40

THE LONELINESS WE ALL FEEL
by David Zahl

*And they heard the sound of the LORD God walking in
the garden in the cool of the day, and the man and his
wife hid themselves from the presence of the LORD.*

Genesis 3:8

Why are we so lonely? And what do we do about our loneliness?
We're in a constant state of connection with people, yet we feel lonelier than we ever have before. What is going on? Loneliness, really,
is simply the desire for intimacy. Loneliness is not synonymous
with being alone or bored, nor does being with others guarantee
protection from loneliness. Anyone who's married knows that.

Why are we so lonely? Well, in theological terms, it has
everything to do with the law of God. The law pushes us toward
ambition and self-actualization, and the price we often pay is
loneliness, a lack of connections. What do we do? We sacrifice
family for career. It reminds me of the great *New Yorker* cartoon of
Abraham looking up at the clouds as he's about to sacrifice Isaac
and saying, "Must I sacrifice family for career?"

We're lonely for some cultural reasons, but we're lonely for reasons that are much more than cultural, because people have always been lonely, and they always will be lonely. We're lonely because there is a shortage of love. We *feel* our aloneness because there is a paucity of grace and an overabundance of judgment. There is a whole lot of law and not a lot of gospel out there. Our isolation, our being cast out of the garden, our division is sin, pure and simple sin, and that sin isolates. The poet George Herbert wrote, "Surely if each one saw another's heart, there would be no commerce, no sale or bargain pass; all would disperse and live apart."[14]

When John Lennon sings, "I am a loser and I'm not who I pretend to be,"[15] this is what he's getting at. Sin isolates; it inspires hiding. We know who we should be but we also know who we are, and so we see how far short we fall of not just God's law but the law of any kind of decency and dignity. And so we hide and we isolate ourselves. We block intimacy. Hiding makes us even lonelier.

Thought to Remember for Today

The only lasting cure for loneliness is to see ourselves as we are in Christ: completely covered by His righteousness and communing together with Him.

HOW WE DEAL WITH LONELINESS
by David Zahl

And the man and his wife hid themselves
from the presence of the LORD.

Genesis 3:8

Another way we try to deal with loneliness is to distract ourselves from it. We keep ourselves busy all the time. One of the great ironies of modern technology is that it was meant to make it so we'd have more leisure time, get our work done faster. But it didn't really work out that way, did it?

We live in a culture where there is no danger whatsoever of people being too lazy. Our problem is that we cannot rest! "Oh, I'm so busy," we say. But what if you weren't busy? What would that say about you? People might think we've got nothing going on.

But distraction and busy-ness are not the only ways we deal with loneliness. Another way we deal with it is to buy people's love. We think, through some kind of relational transaction, that we can make ourselves into someone who is lovable, because we know we're not lovable as we are. So we try to present to the world only a façade we think will get us love, and then we'll feel a little less alone for the moment.

These are all, really, legalistic ways to live. These are legalistic ways to save ourselves from loneliness. They're legalistic, because they are really all forms of control. We think, *If I do these things, I won't have to deal with my loneliness. I can make myself into a person who won't be lonely. I can pay other people to love me as I want myself to be loved.* But these things only compound the loneliness, because, remember, if an idealized form of you is being loved, you don't feel loved because you know you're not that person. This is why social media, for instance, can compound people's loneliness so much, because even when you do have a gazillion online friends, you know the person who is getting all this attention is actually not you, but some projection.

Thought to Remember for Today

Even though we try to handle our loneliness by controlling what people think of us, the truth is that the Lord sees us as we really are and yet loves us immeasurably. We are fully known and fully loved!

A ONE-WAY RELATIONSHIP

by David Zahl

*And they heard the sound of the LORD God walking in
the garden in the cool of the day, and the man and his
wife hid themselves from the presence of the LORD.*

Genesis 3:8

There has been a lot of suicide in the Christian community, and
I don't want to be reductionistic about suicide, as if the cause
always boils down to one single thing. It's very complicated, and
I wouldn't pretend to understand what someone goes through
before they succumb to such despair, but I will say that I think
the suicides of some well-known pastors is an indictment of
American Christianity.

There seems to be a link between these deaths and the wide-
spread teaching that "life transformation took place at salvation
and the power to overcome was inherent in the baptism of the
Holy Spirit."[16] Now, don't mistake me; I'm not saying the Holy
Spirit doesn't come into someone's life and provide change and
power to change, but guarantees of certain kinds of victory are

actually fueling despair, and some pastors become so frustrated that they don't just give up their faith, but their lives.

I'm not disputing the hope of transformation; I'm disputing the guarantee of transformation, because when you guarantee transformation, you often prevent it from actually happening. A person will inevitably pretend to change, all the while getting more and more stuck in that morbid cycle of spiritual pulse-taking, of which some of us are all too familiar. You know, it's true that a plant cannot grow if it's being dug up every five minutes to check its growth. Law and legalism and judgment are dangerous when encountered in a gospel-less vacuum, because to talk about the law without the gospel is to isolate the suffering person even more than they're already isolated.

What is the antidote then? What is the gospel message to those who are lonely? It's a relationship. It's not a theology; it's a Person. But it's not the kind of relationship we tend to have with other people. It's a one-way relationship where you have real freedom because of the assurance that nothing you can do can make God love you any more or any less.

Thought to Remember for Today

It is true that God's salvation is power to change. But it's also true that until we are brought into glory, we will always have sins and struggles. Don't let this reality drive you to despair. God loves you and is patient with you. Remember today that there's nothing you can do or fail to do that will make God love you any less.

SAVED BY THE SAVIOR

by David Zahl

This is love: not that we loved God, but that he loved us and sent his Son as an atoning sacrifice for our sins.

1 John 4:10 NIV

No number of gospel-centered books or conferences or blogs will render grace any less urgent. The climb may be even steeper for those of us who've been brought up on American religious bootstrapping. And so we have to be careful. We have to be careful that we don't turn the important idea of one-way love into a law. We could turn it into a way to measure and control others and ourselves.

A marketing strategy may be able to reference the gospel, but it cannot contain it. The forgiveness of sins is by definition immune to co-option or positioning. Thank God! You can paint grace as the hot new stop on the Christian train all you want, but its reality is another matter. We are saved not by knowledge or theology, but by the Savior. And as much as I wish it weren't so, the stakes are not imaginary—they are real. Suicide is not just a secular phenomenon. The need for forgiveness and grace is universal—people are desperate for it everywhere. And no amount of slick packaging will save them. No amount of "gospel *as concept*" will help them. They don't need big ideas. They need a big Savior! The good news is the gospel *has* intervened; God *has* intervened. "This is love: not that we loved God, but that he loved us and sent his Son as an atoning sacrifice for our sins" (1 John 4:10 NIV).

Grace says you are loved right now. Christian freedom is the freedom to *be* rather than to grow. I have a certain antipathy to the notion that we're getting better and better all the time. And it's so clearly belied by our experience.

Thought to Remember for Today

Saul Bellow wrote, "The forgiveness of sins is perpetual and righteousness first is not required."[17] That is the message of the gospel, not that you must love to get love, but that we have been loved, even in our inability to love, in our unlovableness. And there's something in the message of the forgiveness of sins to offend everybody, except for the person who needs it at the time, which is you, which is me.

NOTHING MORE THAN THE GOSPEL

by Scotty Smith

If, because of one man's trespass, death reigned through
that one man, much more will those who receive the
abundance of grace and the free gift of righteousness
reign in life through the one man Jesus Christ.

Romans 5:17

It's not cliché to say, "There's nothing more than the gospel; there's just more of the gospel." To help you see what I mean, I'm going to share one of my favorite quotes from the *Chronicles of Narnia: The Last Battle.* The children are moving from the Shadowlands into Narnia, and Queen Lucy says, "In our world, too, a Stable once had something inside it that was bigger than our whole world."[18]

That stable is the centerpiece of what we call in church history *Advent.* It is the grand declaration of our God, who is rich in mercy, who knew that the revelation of Himself as Creator could only be surpassed by the revelation of His being revealed as a Redeemer. So He sent Jesus for us. And the stable that seems so small to us is a magnificent metaphor for what the gospel is all about. If, when we speak the word *gospel*, we mean anything other than or less than the person and the work of Jesus, we need an adjustment. That person and work is far more glorious, far more magnificent than we can even imagine.

Let me invite you to follow along with me over the next few days as I share more reflections on this gospel revolution that began in that tiny stable and how this revolutionary power that raised Jesus from the dead on our behalf is truly in our midst today, changing us. Here is a fuller glimpse into the new, expansive world of the gospel of Jesus Christ:

> For if many died through one man's trespass, much more have the grace of God and the free gift by the grace of that one man Jesus Christ abounded for many. And the free gift is not like the result of that one man's sin. For the judgment following one trespass brought condemnation, but the free gift following many trespasses brought justification. For if, because of one man's trespass, death reigned through that one man, much more will those who receive the abundance of grace and the

free gift of righteousness reign in life through
the one man Jesus Christ. (Rom. 5:15–17)

Thought to Remember for Today

As we begin to think more deeply about these words, why not
join me in this prayer:

*Father, Son, and Holy Spirit, glorious triune God, we thank You
that there was a stable in our world that contained something
bigger than the entire universe. May Your commitment through
Jesus and our union with Him expand the horizons of our hearts
that we might live as carriers of Your story. Please show us the
much moreness of this gospel. In Jesus's name and for His glory,
we pray. Amen.*

THE MUCH MORENESS OF GOD'S LOVE

by Scotty Smith

That you, being rooted and grounded in love, may have strength to comprehend … the love of Christ that surpasses knowledge.

Ephesians 3:17–19

I'm discovering the much moreness of God's love. God's lavish love for us in Jesus keeps getting bigger and bigger. And a central dimension of that gospel is the love of God. This is why Paul prayed as he did in Ephesians 3, that we might know the love of God that surpasses knowledge so that we may be filled with the fullness of God.

How in the world can we imagine that prayer being answered? Let me give you one concrete connection in life for what that's been meaning to me over the last few years. I recently, for the first time, publicly articulated my story of experiencing sexual abuse, which I mentioned previously. Yet for so many years, over half a century, I was representative of one who could say with all my heart, "I know for sure that Jesus has died for all my sins, past, present, and future, in word, thought, and deed. Should I die tonight, I have the complete confidence that I will go to heaven because I believe Jesus lived and died in my place." But to understand the power of the love of God to deal with your guilt is one thing; it's another thing to deal with your shame.

In these last few years, the Lord has been taking me deeper into seeing just how much shame has defined my life. There's a big difference between guilt and shame. Guilt would say this: *I did something wrong*. Shame says: *Something is wrong with me*. The voice of guilt: *I need forgiveness*. The voice of shame: *I need to be different*. The voice of guilt: *I failed*. The voice of shame: *I am a failure*. The voice of guilt: *I broke a rule*. The voice of shame: *I am a broken person*. Guilt says, *I made a mistake*; shame says, *I am a mistake*. Guilt: *I didn't do enough*; shame: *I am not enough*.

I want you to know how much of my life—as a married man, as a dad, and as a pastor—shame has been a resounding echo in my heart. I lived enslaved to the kind of shame that told me I have nothing to give other than the gifts God has entrusted to me. But I taste now the freedom of the gospel, which says God loves not simply what I can do for Him, but me. He loves *me*.

Thought to Remember for Today

Perhaps, like me, you might be able to say, "I, by the power of this love, am beginning to realize I have something to offer simply as a person." I want you to know, whatever the shame is, whether or not it is generated out of sexual abuse, Jesus and His love and the much moreness of this gospel are here to meet you now.

Day 46

THE MUCH MORENESS
OF GOD'S HEAVEN

by Scotty Smith

He is before all things, and in him all things hold together.

Colossians 1:17

The older I've grown in this gospel, the more I've come to realize that the gospel has enormous implications. Calvin College professor Nathan Bierma put it like this in a great little book he wrote called *Bringing Heaven Down to Earth*: "The Gospel stands on three legs, not one; Christ's redeeming work was done to restore nature, culture, and human beings. Now, *that's* good news."[19] When we live in the hope of the big gospel, we see Jesus Christ, not just as a serial intruder on people's souls, but the One in whom "all things hold together," in the words of Colossians 1:17.

Bierma continues, *"All things*—not just people's hearts but the infrastructure of nature, culture, and relationships. So the hope of the big gospel is not just going to heaven to be with God, but a vision of the new earth and the heavenly city as the place where God's authority over all of life is made complete. Living in the hope of heaven means seeing glimpses of such a place already, and wanting more."[20] And not only wanting more, but living and loving missionally, because this is the good news of the gospel. It's not merely that we go to heaven when we die; it's that we actually live before we die, and we live with a view to the city whose builder and maker is God (Heb. 11:10).

Not one hair falls from our heads apart from the sovereign decree of the true King, who happens to be the bridegroom who gave Himself for a whore to make her His queen, that we might live together in this very world, this very "hood" to His glory. This world will be made new. As we see this gospel, as we are alive to the love of God, not only for us but also for one another, we are redemptively "careless" about the rest of our days.

God has left nothing to chance, but everything to Christ. And every one of us matters, but none of us is the point. Or as Francis Schaeffer said, "There are no little people and no little places."[21] It means that you don't have to think, *Maybe this will be the day when I really get serious about God and move to Sudan.* I pray some of you will know a calling to move to Sudan, but some of us just need to move across the aisle, move across the street to begin to see Jesus is not making all new *things*, but making all things new.

Thought to Remember for Today

In the gospel, we're characters in the story, because we're the broken rebels and fools Jesus came for. We were triumphed over by the gospel. We are in the train of the true King, who's currently reigning and making all things new, including us.

THE MUCH MORENESS OF THE SON

by Scotty Smith

*Grace to you and peace from him who is
and who was and who is to come.*

Revelation 1:4

The words of Revelation are the words of an octogenarian. The apostle John, one of the original twelve disciples, is writing as an eighty-year-old man on the Isle of Patmos. God gave him a difficult season in his life that then culminated in the series of visions that began to supersize the gospel in John's life. I'm in my mid-sixties and I think, *Lord, if I live to be eighty, can I see what John sees, can I behold like he did, can theology be doxology in my life, can the informed mind be the inflamed heart and the engaged hands until I suck my last breath of oxygen?* John wrote—and it's almost like you're at a wedding party or some event where there's a toast—these wonderful words:

> Grace to you and peace from him who is and
> who was and who is to come, and from the
> seven spirits who are before his throne, and
> from Jesus Christ the faithful witness, the
> firstborn of the dead, and the ruler of kings
> on earth. (Rev. 1:4–5)

Folks, get over your obsession with who is sitting in the White House. It's who is sitting on the throne of heaven that matters. It does not mean we become apolitical, and it certainly doesn't mean we become cynical. It means we love and we serve with hope. John finished out the vision this way:

> To him who loves us and has freed us from
> our sins by his blood and made us a king-
> dom, priests to his God and Father, to him
> be glory and dominion forever and ever.
> Amen. Behold, he is coming with the clouds,
> and every eye will see him, even those who
> pierced him, and all tribes of the earth will
> wail on account of him. Even so. Amen. "I
> am the Alpha and the Omega," says the Lord

God, "who is and who was and who is to
come, the Almighty." (Rev. 1:5–8)

Can you hear it in the heart of an eighty-year-old, wrinkled
man? Can you hear the wonder, the glory, the freedom, the will-
ingness to show up in Rome and to live in this story, to follow
this Jesus? This is the One incarnate with us and for us. This is the
One in whom we share union.

Thought to Remember for Today

Consider the last verse of the Bible and hear the always much
moreness of God's grace for us: "The grace of the Lord Jesus be
with God's people. Amen" (Rev. 22:21 NIV).

THERE IS NO PANIC IN HEAVEN

by Scotty Smith

He who sits in the heavens laughs.

Psalm 2:4

The much moreness of the gospel results not simply in a broader understanding of God's love, but also the much moreness of God's laughter. Here's what I mean by this and why coming alive to the laughter of God and the much moreness of the gospel is rocking my world.

First, I know this is true: I have never been and never will be the fourth member of the Trinity. God does not need me. But He wants me. And folks, when you begin to discover the gospel in that way, it will set you free.

Second, and I say this now as a man in my mid-sixties: there are fewer things I'm absolutely certain about, and there is more appropriate room in my life for not knowing everything. God does all things well, but not all things easy. Listen to Psalm 2:

Why do the nations rage and the peoples plot
in vain? The kings of the earth set themselves,
and the rulers take counsel together, against
the LORD and against his Anointed, saying,
"Let us burst their bonds apart and cast away
their cords from us." He who sits in the heavens laughs; the Lord holds them in derision.
Then he will speak to them in his wrath, and
terrify them in his fury, saying, "As for me, I
have set my King on Zion."

Who is the installed king already? We're not waiting for Jesus
to become King of Kings and Lord of Lords. He already is. Let's
continue in the psalm:

"I have set my King on Zion, my holy hill."
I will tell of the decree: The LORD said to
me, "You are my Son; today I have begotten
you. Ask of me, and I will make the nations
your heritage, and the ends of the earth your
possession. You shall break them with a rod
of iron and dash them in pieces like a potter's
vessel." Now therefore, O kings, be wise;

be warned, O rulers of the earth. Serve the
LORD with fear, and rejoice with trembling.
Kiss the Son, lest he be angry, and you perish
in the way, for his wrath is quickly kindled.
Blessed are all who take refuge in him.

Thought to Remember for Today

This psalm is directed to the people of God, voiced out to the
nations of the world. In it, the world is seemingly out of control
and evil seems to be prevailing. But there's no panic in heaven,
friends. As Steve Brown has said, there is no perspiration on the
top lip of the mouth of God. Our God is in control and our God
loves us.

OUR AMNESIA EPIDEMIC

by Paul David Tripp

*The L*ORD *is my light and my salvation.*

Psalm 27:1

A plague has infected the church of the Lord Jesus Christ. It's a sad disease. It's left us weakened and broken and discouraged and afraid. It's almost like as soon as you come to faith in Jesus Christ, you get infected. And it robs you of your spiritual vitality. It robs you of your joy. It robs you of the rest that Jesus died for you to have. It reduces you to timidity and doubt and worry and dark addictions of all kinds. It somehow, someway, gets us all. The problem is that most people don't know they have it. They actually live with the delusion that they're healthy when everything in their life points to the fact that they're sick.

What is this disease, you ask? It's "identity amnesia." We have forgotten who we are. And in forgetting who we are, we frantically look for identity in thousands of places where it will never be found, places where you were never meant to look for identity. You probably do it so instinctively, so frequently, and so naturally that you don't actually know you're doing it. You're so used to carrying the burden that you don't know you're carrying the burden anymore. You're spiritual back has hurt you for so long, you've forgotten that you're in pain.

Now, I say this all the time and I'm going to continue to say it, because I think it's important to say: you are in a constant conversation with yourself. No one's more influential in your life than you are, because no one talks to you more than you do. And a principal part of that conversation is this conversation of identity. You're constantly saying things to you about you. You are always assigning to yourself some kind of identity. And the identity you assign to yourself will somehow, someway, set the course for how you deal with literally everything in your life. You never escape the identity you assign to yourself, ever. It's always forming the way you're interacting, even with the most mundane things in your existence.

Thought to Remember for Today

As you begin to consider your true identity in Christ, you can rest in the reality that the Lord is with you, working to reveal His work in and to you, and that even though you may struggle, He has promised to complete His work.

WHAT GOD IS IN TIMES OF TROUBLE

by Paul David Tripp

The LORD is my light and my salvation.

Psalm 27:1

Let's look again at Psalm 27. What I love about this psalm is that it's a psalm of trouble. It is perhaps in moments of trouble when your true sense of identity gets most exposed. What you're really looking to—to give you rest, peace, security, and that inner sense of meaning—will always be exposed in moments of trouble.

This psalm was probably penned by David when he was either hiding out from Saul or fleeing from his own son, Absalom, who was conspiring to take his throne. Here are the first five verses of the psalm:

> The LORD is my light and my salvation; whom shall I fear? The LORD is the stronghold of my life; of whom shall I be afraid? When evildoers assail me to eat up my flesh, my adversaries

and foes, it is they who stumble and fall.
Though an army encamp against me, my
heart shall not fear; though war arise against
me, yet I will be confident. One thing have I
asked of the LORD, that will I seek after: that
I may dwell in the house of the LORD all the
days of my life, to gaze upon the beauty of the
LORD and to inquire in his temple. For he will
hide me in his shelter in the day of trouble; he
will conceal me under the cover of his tent;
he will lift me high upon a rock. (Ps. 27:1–5)

It's very interesting that this psalm of trouble doesn't begin
with trouble, but with theology. True rest in trouble is rooted in
sound theology. It's these truths that begin to tell me how to think
of my place in this world. The Lord is light; the Lord is salvation;
the Lord is a stronghold. Think about what those metaphors
point to. The Lord is light. Light in Scripture is that which is
pure and holy and just and true. The Lord is salvation. He is the
One who delivers me from evil, evil internal and evil external.
The Lord is a stronghold—the picture of a fortified city, a place
of retreat, a place of rest, a place of safety. Yes, there is One who
provides safety.

Thought to Remember for Today

In whatever you may be facing today, you can rest knowing that the Lord is your light, your salvation, your fortified city. You are not alone and He is not weak. He is with you and knows everything you are facing, and—best of all—He loves you.

THE LORD IS *MY* LIGHT AND *MY* SALVATION

by Paul David Tripp

The LORD is my light and my salvation.

Psalm 27:1

Think with me about what David said in this beautiful psalm. David didn't say the Lord is light. He didn't say the Lord is salvation. He didn't say the Lord is a stronghold, did he? He qualified these nouns with the word *my*, and that changes everything.

Enough of abstract, impersonal, distant, isolated, informational theology! It's not the theology of the Word of God. It doesn't help us; it hurts us. I don't need more ideas rattling around in my brain. I've got way more than I can think about already. Half the time I'm confused.

You see, the theology of the Word of God, properly understood, never just defines who God is. It redefines who you are as His children. And that two-letter word *my* makes all the difference in the world. The Lord is *my* light. This righteousness that exists by grace has been unleashed on me. It's *my* righteousness by grace. I could've never earned it; I could've never deserved it.

As a poor, zealous seminary student, I was exegeting my way through Romans. I had gotten a big legal pad and cut the corners off every other page. And I had actually taken the page out of my Greek New Testament and glued it there so you could see the Greek from both sides. And I was writing copious theological notes. I got to about Romans 7 or 8, and it hit me that I had spent what seemed like endless hours studying Paul's letter to the Romans, and I had not been touched by it at all. It had been solely an idea exercise. I was a theo-geek. I prided myself in understanding all the labyrinthine theology in that passage, but it did nothing for me and I began to weep.

The Lord is my salvation. I'm saved. Me, this dark man with all those selfish, evil thoughts, with all my self-aggrandizing behavior, with all my wanting to be sovereign over my own life, salvation has burst into *my* life. I'm saved, I'm saved, I'm saved!

Thought to Remember for Today

Listen, you don't hope in justification; you hope in a Savior who justifies you. Jesus didn't purchase save-ability; He took names to the cross. You don't find life in the abstract concept of salvation, but in a God who willingly sacrificed Himself to save you.

WHERE DO YOU FIND YOUR IDENTITY?

by Paul David Tripp

The LORD is my light and my salvation.

Psalm 27:1

Think about where we look for identity. How about in relationships? How many of us put burdens on relationships that they can't bear because we're getting our identity out of how that relationship is faring? It just never works. Many spouses have said to me that all they ever wanted was a husband or a wife who would make them happy. I'm thinking, *Are you crazy? You actually think this person has the ability to be the source—the lasting, sturdy, continual source—of your happiness? Who in the world do you think you've married? The fourth member of the Trinity?*

Or we find our identity in possessions. Let's say that, in ways you don't realize, you've attached your identity, meaning, and purpose to the order, beauty, and cleanliness of your home. Now, what is that going to create? Well, you're going to be just an incessantly uptight person. You will notice crumbs on the kitchen counter that weren't there before and it will break your heart. And you wonder, why would they do this to me? Or you'll follow people into rooms, making sure they don't make that room look like somebody actually lives there.

I'll make the confession. I've been married for forty-two years, and I'm an Ephesians 5 failure. I can be so easily irritated. I want to be agreed with. I don't ask much of Luella: just always say, "You're absolutely right." It doesn't seem that hard.

Or we try to get our identity in achievements. How many times do you do something for somebody that they didn't notice, and you have to find a way of letting them know you did it for them? Or maybe you're more spiritual. Maybe you have determined that you're going to be the smartest person theologically in the room at all times. You have committed yourself to theological "always-right-ism," because that's where you get your sense of identity.

The antidote to all this is to see who we are through the lens of God's Word and see in that Word what He's done for us.

Thought to Remember for Today

The first verse of Psalm 27 is the only place where identity will ever be found. The Lord is *my* light. The Lord is *my* salvation. The Lord is *my* stronghold. The theology of the Word of God is never impersonal; it's deeply personal. It radically rearranges everything in my existence, because my life has been invaded by this awesome grace. A Savior has come to me and I am okay. Praise Him!

GAZING UPON THE BEAUTY OF THE LORD

by Paul David Tripp

One thing have I asked of the LORD, that will I seek after: that I may dwell in the house of the LORD all the days of my life, to gaze upon the beauty of the LORD.

Psalm 27:4

Let's continue in Psalm 27:2–4:

> When evildoers assail me to eat up my flesh, my adversaries and foes, it is they who stumble and fall. Though an army encamp against me, my heart shall not fear; though war rise against me, yet I will be confident. One thing have I asked of the LORD, and that will I seek after: that I may dwell in the house of the LORD all the days of my life, to gaze upon the beauty of the LORD.

Put yourself in this situation. If you actually had an army encamping against you, what would the one thing be that you would ask of the Lord? Think about that. How about weapons? How about asking God to just incinerate them? But look at what David actually said in this dark situation: "One thing have I asked of the LORD ... that I may dwell in the house of the LORD ... to gaze upon the beauty of the LORD." Now, either David was so super-spiritual that none of us can relate to him, or he was onto something wonderful here.

David knew Someone exists who is of such awesome, gorgeous, glorious beauty that He is way more beautiful than any ugly thing David would ever face in his life. Furthermore, he knew grace had connected him to this beauty.

None of the things that get you down is ultimate. God's beauty is ultimate. You must look at yourself through the lens of the gorgeous, glorious beauty of the grace of the One who is light, life, salvation, and refuge, because it is only then that your heart will find rest.

Thought to Remember for Today

Let me encourage you to *gaze*; to start each day with your Bible and do nothing but gaze upon the beauty of the Lord. The Lord is my light. The Lord is my salvation. The Lord is my stronghold. Now, hear the rhetorical question, "Of whom should I be afraid?" What's the answer? No one, nothing.

THE COST OF ONE-WAY LOVE

by Elyse Fitzpatrick

… delivered up for our trespasses and raised for our justification.

Romans 4:25

Let's think about what it cost Jesus to love us, because this wonderful, one-way love does not come to us free. It's free to us, of course, but it wasn't free for Him. The second person of the Trinity, who always existed in joy and light, left His Father's home and gestated in the womb of a little virgin girl in a hick village. In darkness, He grew just like you. He had to learn language. He had to learn table manners. And He had to go with His father to the synagogue to learn the Word. He didn't access His deity to make it easy for Himself, so that He could just automatically memorize passages. He didn't hit a home run every time He played ball. He was completely weak in all the ways you and I are weak.

And after He fasted for forty days, the Bible says He was hungry. Now, why does the Bible tell us that? The writers of the Bible wanted us to remember that Jesus was a human. Because we need a perfect representative. We need someone who is human like us to fulfill all the law. He fulfills all the law in our place, so that as God's perfect sacrifice that takes away the sin of the world, He could die the substitutionary death for us so that we can be justified.

If the gospel doesn't hold the center of your life, if God's one-way love isn't what defines you, captivates you, and motivates you, then it's going to be something else. It will be homeschooling, which is fine, or it will be politics or it will be gender roles or career or sports or *whatever*. Something will fill the void that should only be filled by the gospel.

The gospel must hold the center of your life. And the only way it can do that is by you saying, "God help me remember the price You paid. Help me remember the incredible cost paid by Your Son."

Thought to Remember for Today

I've got to take myself back to the gospel over and over and over and over again, and I've got to pray, "God, help me remember. Help me remember that Your law has already been fulfilled and Your death has wiped away all my guilt. Lord, help me." You need to do this too. And the joy is, by praying it, we're remembering it!

Day 55

THE FRUIT OF ONE-WAY LOVE: TRANSPARENCY

by Elyse Fitzpatrick

He denied it with an oath: "I do not know the man."

Matthew 26:72

I think I know why most of you are reading this devotional. I think you're reading this because you're hoping against hope that there is still someplace in the world where you can get good news. You're hoping the message you heard when you first came to Christ—that you're forgiven and made new—is still true and is still your story. I'm sure some of you are parched souls looking for a cup of cold water.

There is great good news in God's one-way love for you. And part of that good news is that you can live transparently. Are you glad the story of Peter's denial is in the Bible? Now, is it a good thing that Peter sinned and denied Christ? No, of course not. Is it a good thing that we know about it? Yes, of course it is. So why are we not transparent more often? I think it's because we're surrounded by people who pretend that everything in their life is perfect and we've all entered into this unspoken pact to pretend together. But all this pretending will only result in despair or pride.

I want to be transparent with you about the fact that I'm a mess. I used to think that after forty-some years of life, I would be better than this. (I'm sure my husband thinks the same thing!) And you might be thinking, *Oh, she's not really that big of a mess; she's just saying that.* I hope that's what you're thinking, but it's not true. I am that big of a mess. I'm a sinner, and I swear to you, the further along I get in the Christian journey, the more sinful I see my heart is. But I am at the same time growing in the courage to be honest about that. Because the good news is that while I see more and more of my own sinfulness each new day, I also see more and more of God's grace. Neither my sin nor yours can "scare off" God.

Thought to Remember for Today

The fruit of being loved the way I've been loved, in spite of all my unbelief, idolatry, selfishness, demandingness, irritability, worry, and anger, is that I am finally willing, at least a little bit, to stop pretending. The truth is that I am broken, and my guess is that you are too, and that's why you're reading this. Just say (out loud, maybe?), "I'm broken, but He loves me."

REMEMBER ME

by Elyse Fitzpatrick

Remember me.

Luke 23:42

I've come to the conclusion that there are really only three kinds of people in the world, and they were all represented there by those miserable creatures hanging on Golgotha's mount. There they were, hands and feet pinioned to wood, naked, shamed, in excruciating agony, with no hope of anything other than hours that would seem like a millennia, waiting while the life drained out of them. Two of them faced a reality that they had made a mistake from which they would never recover. And one of them hung there dying out of love for hopeless wretches who have about as much ability to changes themselves as those other two men hanging on the cross.

One of them is angry. He says, "If you're so great, then why don't you get up off the cross and help me." (Now, I'm going to be really honest: there are days in my life when I've been like that.) And then there is someone else there on a cross who is begging for mercy. He says to the angry man, "Why don't you just shut up? I've been listening to people like you talk about injustice in the world my whole life, and now we're finally getting justice." And in his pain and helplessness and hopelessness, the man mutters these words to Jesus: "Remember me" (Luke 23:42). Then, in the most astounding demonstration of one-way love, God washes that poor, wretched soul.

Remember me. That's all we've got.

And then, the last one of the three hanging there on Golgotha had already done His begging. He had already asked that there might be some other way for Him to free us from the condemnation we deserved. And God gave Him grace and strength, not in His deity, but in His humanity, to stand. Think of the love that worked in the heart of that forsaken, doubting, human man, who was at that moment walking by faith and not by sight, who in His humanity said, "My God, my God, why have You forsaken me?" That wasn't a rhetorical question. It was your Savior suffering in your place so that you would never be deserted, so you would never be exiled, so you would never be isolated.

Thought to Remember for Today

What does the fruit of one-way love look like? It looks like the ability to be transparent and to say, "I have nothing except 'remember me.' And the only reason I have that is because You gave it to me."

Day 57

RESTING IN GOD

by Elyse Fitzpatrick

Sing aloud, O daughter of Zion; shout, O Israel!
Rejoice and exult with all your heart. … The LORD
has taken away the judgments against you.

Zephaniah 3:14–15

The more you trust the gospel, the more rest there will be in your soul. Oh my, we live such frenetic lives, trying and trying and trying to prove things to ourselves (and others): *I'm not like my mom; I'm not like my parents; I'm better than you; I've got my act together; I'm winning the world for Christ.* This whole frenetic, stressed out, grumpy approach to life has got to go. We just need some rest.

I love this passage from Zephaniah 3. "Sing aloud, O daughter of Zion; shout, O Israel!" You know why we don't shout and sing? We don't rejoice because we're usually working so hard and becoming so terribly miserable. But listen to these words:

> The LORD has taken away the judgments against you; he has cleared away your enemies.

> The King of Israel, the LORD, is in your midst;
> you shall never again fear evil. On that day it
> shall be said to Jerusalem: "Fear not, O Zion;
> let not your hands grow weak. The LORD your
> God is in your midst, a mighty one who will
> save; he will rejoice over you with gladness; he
> will quiet you by his love; he will exult over
> you with loud singing." (Zeph. 3:15–17)

This passage doesn't say He will mourn over you with disappointment because you're such losers. Listen, *God is not disappointed in you.* And I can say that, because disappointment is always a by-product of unmet expectations. God has no unmet expectations when it comes to you. All His expectations for righteousness have been completely fulfilled and all His expectations for your debt—they've been fulfilled too. He's not disappointed. He says, "I will quiet you by My love; I will exult over you with loud singing."

I'm very sure taking on more guilt about what you're failing to do won't result in more obedience. That hasn't worked very well so far, has it? So have a nice afternoon. Have a nice life. Better yet, have a nice eternity. You can relax now and stop pretending.

You can rest because the work of salvation is accomplished by Christ and God delights in you!

Thought to Remember for Today

The Lord has taken away the judgments against you! He is rejoicing over you with gladness. The Lord has promised to bless and keep you. His face is smiling on you now, and He will be gracious to you today and forever! He sees you, He's watching over you, and He's rejoicing.

Day 58

A POOL ELEPHANTS CAN SWIM IN

by Steve Brown

*Are not two sparrows sold for a penny? And not one of
them will fall to the ground apart from your Father.
But even the hairs of your head are all numbered.*

Matthew 10:29–30

I lived during the Jesus movement. That was an awakening that
was as great as those occurring under the ministries of George
Whitefield and Jonathan Edwards. And it was a wonderful time.
I didn't know what to do with all those kids who were coming
into our church, getting baptized and going out with a joy that
was infectious, a freedom that scared the spit out of so many other
Christians. Those kinds of things only last a generation or two,
and we're running out of gasoline. I've said, "Oh God, it would
be really cool if I could hang around and see You do it one more
time. Do it again. Do it again." And He is.

You may be a part of the beginning of something that is
going to shake America to its roots. You don't have a thing to
defend; you don't have anything to fake. You're announcing to the

world that you're screwed up and Jesus likes you a lot. That dog will hunt, and I'm so glad to be a part of it.

Not too long ago, I was working on this material and it was very early in the morning. And I was thinking about the subject "everyday grace." *What in the world am I going to say about everyday grace?* At that moment, my elbow hit a glass of water on my desk and knocked it over. The water fell on writing, on my computer keyboard, and on my pants before the glass fell to the floor. I looked like I needed Depends. So what did I do? I kicked that glass across my office. I picked up the papers and threw them in the air and said words that ought never proceed from the mouth of an ordained individual. And in the middle of my cussing and my spitting and drying myself off, I heard laughter. Nobody gets up as early as I do, so I knew it wasn't staff. It was angels.

And I found a principle there that I want to teach you: if you don't live in God's grace when you spill water, you won't live in God's grace when you get cancer. This is not a doctrine so much as it is life.

Thought to Remember for Today

If grace doesn't work when you go to the bathroom, it won't work with your sin. If it doesn't work when you're making love to your wife or your husband, it won't work when your life falls apart.

Grace is a pool where elephants can swim and children can play. It has to do with reading a good book and going to a movie and falling on your knees in repentance and rejoicing in worship. Grace isn't just a doctrine; it's a 24-7 context for living.

OF BALD HEADS AND DEAD BIRDS

by Steve Brown

Are not two sparrows sold for a penny? And not one of
them will fall to the ground apart from your Father.
But even the hairs of your head are all numbered.

Matthew 10:29–30

Ponder these incredible, provocative words from our Lord:

> So have no fear of them, for nothing is
> covered that will not be revealed, or hidden
> that will not be known. What I tell you in
> the dark, say in the light, and what you hear
> whispered, proclaim on the housetops. And
> do not fear those who kill the body but can-
> not kill the soul. Rather fear him who can
> destroy both soul and body in hell. Are not
> two sparrows sold for a penny? And not one
> of them will fall to the ground apart from
> your Father. But even the hairs of your head

are all numbered. Fear not, therefore; you are
of more value than many sparrows. So everyone who acknowledges me before men, I will
also acknowledge before my Father who is in
heaven, but whoever denies me before men,
I will also deny before my Father who is in
heaven. (Matt. 10:26–33)

Please note the easy way Jesus moves from the macrocosm
to the microcosm, from the big deal about eternity and about
salvation to "little things" like birds and bald heads. As I read this
passage, I think, *Man, that is a big jump.* And then I remember
that if you don't live in grace in the little things, you won't live in
grace in the big things. Listen, God is involved in bald heads and
dead sparrows and the eternal verities of the Christian faith.

Michel Quoist, in his book simply titled *Prayers,* writes a lot
about what we might call "colloquial prayers." He writes prayers
about almost everything he experienced, and that's the joy of that
little book. When he sinned, he said, "I'm ashamed of being seen
by my friends, I'm ashamed of being seen by you, Lord…. Lord,
don't look at me like that, for I am naked, I am dirty, I am down."
And God said, "Come, son, look up…. It's not falling that is the
worst, but staying on the ground."[22]

But one of the more fun prayers is where Quoist is sitting in church behind a bald-headed guy. And he's thinking about Jesus' words that even the hairs of your head are numbered. And he's thinking, *God, I praise you for that dome. I praise you that it's so smooth. And I think of Jesus' words, "Not a hair falls unless God's aware of it." God, you've thought about this man a whole lot.* That makes me laugh, but it also comforts me.

Thought to Remember for Today

The good news doesn't just cover us in church; it covers us in every place we go and in everything we do. It plays in the little arenas of falling hairs and dead birds.

Day 60

ONE-WAY LOVE: THE ONLY ANTIDOTE FOR *ACEDIA*

by Steve Brown

Are not two sparrows sold for a penny? And not one of them will fall to the ground apart from your Father.

Matthew 10:29

I have a friend named Jeff who is HIV-positive. He struggles with same-sex attraction. He grew up in a condemning home, and although I've never met him face-to-face, I dedicated one of my books to him. I dedicated a book to him because I love him a lot. And one day I got an email from him. I had done a teaching series once on the subject of *acedia*. You may not have the foggiest idea what acedia is, but it's one of the seven deadly sins, the one sometimes translated as "sloth." But acedia is more than sloth. It's that demonic sense of futility and hopelessness when you just don't want to do this anymore. Well, Jeff heard this teaching series, and this is what he wrote to me:

> I've been listening to those CDs Key Life sent me over the last few weeks, dealing with

acedia. I have to admit, when I first saw what
they were about, I was reluctant to listen.
Coming from where I do, I assumed you
would be discussing how to get the fire back,
how to stir up the old passion by reading
more of the Bible, going to church every
Wednesday and Sunday and praying twice in
the morning, once at lunch, and just before
bed. I figured you would discuss our laziness,
our lack of passion and condemn us for not
returning Christ's gift to us with undying
faithfulness. And perhaps all of those things
need to be said, and they are, of course, true.
But after hearing it so much for so long, I
can't deal with being beat over the head anymore. I do enough of that to myself. I know
all too well that I need to get better. Dealing
with my issues, acedia is not only impossi-
ble to avoid, it surrounds my heart and it's
exceedingly difficult to feel any passion when
you don't feel worthy to be loved or accepted
by a holy God. It's hard to dance before the
Lord when you think he only thinks bad

thoughts toward you because you still haven't gotten the victory.

I remember once, my wife, Anna, had had a miserable week. Everything had gone wrong: things had broken in the house, the cat had brought a mouse in, and she wasn't feeling well. She'd had to see the doctor and was on antibiotics. Now, if you're a guy, you think your job is to fix things. Well, I wanted to fix my wife, and so I started making suggestions. And she said, "Honey, I don't want you to fix me; I want you to hug me." Sometimes I say that to God.

Thought to Remember for Today

Do you know the Lord is not expecting you to "get the victory"? He already got it for you through His Son. He wants you to repent of your sin, yes, but if you trust in Jesus, He's not disappointed in you. He knows what a mess you are. And He loves you.

NOTES

1. Martin Luther, *On Christian Liberty*, Facets Series (Minneapolis, MN: Fortress Press, 2003), 65.

2. Justin S. Holcomb, *On the Grace of God* (Wheaton, IL: Crossway, 2013).

3. C. S. Lewis, *The Weight of Glory* (New York: HarperCollins, 2001), 21.

4. "Dr. Ashley Null on Thomas Cranmer," Anglican Church League, www.acl.asn.au/resources/dr-ashley-null-on-thomas-cranmer/.

5. Wright Thompson, "Urban Meyer Will Be Home for Dinner," *ESPN*.com, August 22, 2012, http://espn.go.com/espn/otl/story/_/id/8239451/ohio -state-coach-urban-meyer-new-commitment-balancing-work-family-life.

6. Robert Kolb, Timothy J. Wengert, eds., "Apology of the Augsburg Confession XXI," *The Book of Concord: The Confessions of the Evangelical Lutheran Church*, trans. Charles Arand et al. (Minneapolis, MN: Fortress, 2000), 240.

7. W. H. Auden, "In Praise of Limestone," *Collected Poems*, ed. Edward Mendelson (London: Vintage, 1991), 540.

8. George Whitefield, *Select Sermons of George Whitefield* (Edinburgh: The Banner of Truth Trust, 1997), 81-83.

9. William Beveridge, *Private Thoughts* (London: W. Taylor, 1720), 52.

10. Augustus M. Toplady, "Rock of Ages." (Public Domain.)

11. Jean Calvin, *The Institutes of the Christian Religion* (London: Westminster, 1960), 2:108.

12. Mark Ellingsen, *Reclaiming Our Roots* (Harrisburg, PA: Trinity, 1999), 2:53.

13. Ben Toh, "The King, the Carrot, and the Horse," ubfriends.org, www.ubfriends.org/2011/12/14/the-king-the-carrot-and-the-horse.

14. George Herbert, *The Complete English Poems*, ed. John Tobin (London: Penguin Books, 2005), 119.

15. John Lennon, "I'm a Loser," *Beatles '65* © 1965 Capitol Records.

16. Ted Haggard, "Suicide, Evangelism, and Sorrow," *The Pastor's Pen* (blog), December 12, 2013, tedhaggardblog.com/2013/12/12/suicide-evangelicalism -and-sorrow/.

17. Saul Bellow, *Henderson the Rain King* (London: Penguin Books, 2012), 1.

18. C. S. Lewis, *The Last Battle* (New York: HarperCollins, 2002), 177.

19. Nathan L. K. Bierma, *Bringing Heaven Down to Earth: Connecting This Life to the Next* (Philipsburg, NJ: P&R Publishing, 2005), 137.

20. Bierma, *Bringing Heaven Down to Earth*, 137.

21. Francis A. Schaeffer, *No Little People* (Wheaton, IL: Crossway, 2003), 32.

22. Michel Quoist, *Prayers*, trans. Agnes M. Forsyth and Anne Marie de Commaille (Lanham, MD: Sheed and Ward, 1999), 136–37.